CLAY AND WHEBLE'S

MODERN
MERCHANT BANKING

A GUIDE TO THE WORKINGS

OF THE

ACCEPTING HOUSES OF THE CITY OF LONDON

AND THEIR SERVICES TO

INDUSTRY AND COMMERCE

SECOND EDITION

EDITED BY

C. J. J. CLAY

AND

B. S. WHEBLE
C.B.E., Hon. F.I.B., B.Com.(Lond.)

REVISED BY

THE HON. L. H. L. COHEN
M.A. (Oxon.)

WOODHEAD-FAULKNER · CAMBRIDGE

Woodhead-Faulkner Limited
17 Market Street
Cambridge CB2 3PA

First published 1976
Second edition 1983

ISBN 0 85941 215 6 (Paper)
ISBN 0 85941 216 4 (Cased)

Design by Geoff Green

Typeset by Goodfellow & Egan Phototypesetting, Cambridge

Printed in Great Britain by
St Edmundsbury Press, Bury St Edmunds, Suffolk

PREFACE TO THE SECOND EDITION

Until the publication of the first edition of *Modern Merchant Banking* in 1976, there appears to have been no book that could fairly be claimed to define and describe "merchant banking" and none that could claim to provide a practical definition of the accepting houses or to describe their origin or their work in any detail.

This book was prepared to fill the gap and explain how the accepting houses came into being and what their functions were and now are. It was and is intended to be of particular use to businessmen in the United Kingdom and overseas who may be interested in the services provided by the accepting houses; to colleges and universities throughout the world; to graduates and others who join the staffs of the accepting houses; and to all who wish to study the origins and growth of the City of London as the principal merchanting and banking centre of the world.

The historical material contained in the early chapters is in sketch form to provide the scenario for the later chapters which describe, in some detail, the present-day functions of the houses. Readers will, it is hoped, find enough material in the early chapters to tempt them to search in the great mass of historical literature available to them to complete their knowledge of what lies behind the sketch, and a list of suggested reading is given in Appendix E at the end of the book.

The chapters following Chapter 5 were all written by experts in their own subjects and these chapters have all been revised by professionals for this second edition. They were and are submitted anonymously, but they are endorsed by the editor of the second edition who, like his predecessors, the editors of the first edition, is grateful to such experts for their contributions.

Many factors have made a second edition of *Modern Merchant Banking* essential. The most important of these are the enactment of the *Banking Act, 1979;* the abolition of exchange control; changes in the Bank of England's List of Recognised Banks and in its policy of using acceptances as a main instrument of monetary control; changes in the composition of the Accepting Houses Committee itself; changes within ARIEL; changes in the market place, such as the development of the Unlisted Securities Market, the emergence of floating rate notes as financial instruments and of "bulldog issues" in the international bond market and new practices in the provision of export finance; the enquiry and report of the Wilson Committee; and further developments in self-regulation in the City. All these factors have caused many amendments to be made to the first edition and some sections to be rewritten.

These chapters still emphasise that the accepting houses are required to be professionals at the work they perform; that they are vital to the maintenance of London as the premier financial centre of the world; that they have overseas, as well as domestic, experience second to none; and that they play an important part in earning, and in channelling for the benefit of the nation, the "invisible" income of the United Kingdom on which the country's economy is so dependent.

NOTES ON THE EDITORS

Charles Clay retired from the board of Antony Gibbs & Sons, Limited, at the end of 1970 after 38 years' service with that company which he represented on the Accepting Houses Committee for a long period. He was the first Director-General of the Accepting Houses Committee, holding that office from 1971 until he retired in 1976.

He served for 12 years as a member of the Public Works Loan Board and for five years as a member of the Advisory Council of the Export Credits Guarantee Department. In 1972 he was appointed a member of the Council of the Confederation of British Industry and in 1973 a member of the Executive Committee of the British Bankers' Association. He was Chairman of Automated Real-time Investments Exchange Ltd (ARIEL) from its incorporation until 1982.

Bernard Wheble retired in 1972 from the board of the accepting house Brown, Shipley & Co. Limited, having served with that company for 49 years. For many years he was Chairman of the Technical Committee of the accepting houses and their representative on the International Chamber of Commerce.

In 1963 he was appointed Chairman of the I.C.C. Commission on Banking Technique and Practice. He played a leading part in redrafting the code of practice for documentary credits, standardising documentary credit forms and drafting the code for documentary collections.

He was a member of the Council of the Institute of Bankers for many years. In 1972 he received the rare distinction of Honorary Fellowship of the Institute for his contribution to the practice of banking in the international field.

He is a member of the United Kingdom Simplification of International Trade Procedures Board (SITPRO), serving as Chairman of its Policy Group on Procedures and Documentation.

In 1972 he was awarded the C.B.E. for services to international trade.

L. H. L. (Tim) Cohen was a director of the accepting house M. Samuel & Co. Limited and then Hill Samuel & Co. Limited for 15 years until 1976, when he succeeded Charles Clay as Director-General of the Accepting Houses Committee. He has been a director of ARIEL for six years and is presently its Chairman. He has served on the Executive Committee of the British Bankers' Association and as a member of the Council of the Confederation of British Industry. He was a practising barrister for 12 years.

CONTENTS

Structure of the balance sheet. Bank of England
deposit requirements. Asset management.
Duties of the chief dealer.

PART FOUR: OTHER SERVICES OF THE ACCEPTING HOUSES

PART ONE

THE SCOPE AND DEVELOPMENT OF MERCHANT BANKING

1

INTRODUCTION

In geographical terms, the City of London is restricted to the north bank of the River Thames and is bounded to the east by Aldgate and Bishopsgate (but including the westernmost warehousing area); to the north by Aldersgate and Moorgate and to the west (nowadays) by a roughly north–south line incorporating the Law Courts, Fleet Street and Hatton Garden – but formerly by Ludgate. In civic terms the City is represented by the Lord Mayor and Commonalty of the City of London. Metaphorically, however, "The City" has become synonymous with the conglomerate of institutions which comprise the financial centre in which they operate. Headed by the Bank of England, they are the accepting houses; the clearing banks; the discount houses; the other banks (home and overseas); the issuing houses; the investment trusts; The Stock Exchange; the unit trusts; the Corporation of Lloyd's; the insurance companies; the shipping and commodity exchanges and the London International Financial Futures Exchange and other futures exchanges. It is not the purpose of this book to attempt to define the operations of any of these principal participants other than the accepting houses.

But before doing that, a few paragraphs describing the origins of the City of London and its banking institutions will perhaps help the reader to acclimatise and orientate himself.

Some researchers believe that Celtic Britain boasted a small fortress – with a name that may have sounded like *Lyn-din* – on a northern tributary of the Thames later called the Wall brook.

Other historians consider that, having regard to the oak forests and thick scrub which covered the area, anything larger than small farming communities would have been unlikely, if not impossible.

Of course the level of the land on which London now stands is very much higher than it was in the first century – rebuilding and the infilling of low-lying areas has seen to that – but another factor has changed the situation of London and has made archaeological studies somewhat haphazard. The whole of south-eastern England has sunk so as to result in the tidal length of the Thames being greatly increased: in fact, the high-water level is now some 12 to 14 feet above its level in the first century.

So, in those early days, the Thames to the west of the Wall brook was certainly shallow enough, at low water, to be forded by the Romans when they invaded from the south and reached the Thames in or around A.D. 43. The area of the Wall brook found favour with them and they built Londinium there and used it not only as a point of entry for their supplies by sea, but also for the exports of the indigenous products of England, in particular lead, wool, skins and cloth.

Within 300 years Londinium had become one of the most important cities of the Roman Empire and was enclosed by a great stone wall, large sections of which can still be seen both above and below ground. But as the Roman Empire decayed so did the trading station of Londinium, which became virtually deserted by the Romans by the middle of the fifth century.

Of the years after the Roman occupation of Britain, through the Saxon era and until the Norman period there is not much historical record of the life and business of the City of London but, by the time of the arrival of William the Conqueror in the eleventh century, a new township was springing up, within the old walls, and trade was being redeveloped with Europe and the East. London was becoming a city of merchants, as it was before and has effectively remained ever since; and we are constantly reminded of that as, in this generation, we move around the City – the names of the streets still reflecting the flourishing markets (or "cheaps") of those days, for example Eastcheap, Cheapside, Bread Street, Milk Street, Fish Street Hill, Cornhill, Lime Street and many others.

William the Conqueror borrowed heavily from the Jewish community – which had, as the money-lenders of Europe, developed a settlement in London (streets such as Jewry Street and Old Jewry in the City doubtless being named after them) – and began a vast building programme of cathedrals and castles, some of which give the sightseer pleasure today as permanent memorials of the Norman era.

During the late thirteenth century, after a period of persecution, the Jews were largely banished from England and replaced by the Italian bankers, the Lombards, who arrived from Genoa, Venice and Florence and who became London's principal money-lenders and bankers, giving their name to Lombard Street and laying the foundations for much of our present banking system.

A few centuries later, rudimentary banking experienced a further development through the goldsmiths, who set up shop in Cheapside: they bought bullion, both for their own account and for customers, and issued "notes" in respect of it, the right to the bullion passing with the "note" as it changed hands. But banking as we know it today, the taking of deposits and the making of advances, only emerged after Charles I, failing to get the grants of finance he needed from Parliament, sequestrated some £200,000 of the City merchants' money which was lodged with the Royal Mint, then housed in the Tower of London – and after Charles II borrowed £1.3 million from the Exchequer to fight the War of the Grand Alliance, upon which interest payments were, incidentally, not made for 18 years, leaving the bankers the poorer both in capital and in income. As a clear result of these events, the Bank of England was founded in 1694 under a Royal Charter from William and Mary, in return for a loan of £1.2 million made to the Crown. It was formed, following pleas from the City merchants, to limit and regularise the imposts made by the Crown on the community and, among other business, to maintain the accounts of the merchants and to act as custodians of their growing wealth.

The Bank of England was one of the earliest central banks to be formed in the world – the Bank of Amsterdam in Holland was the first – but it only subsequently developed its role as banker to the Government, note-issuer and lender of last resort to the banking sector, thus to become an important element in the negotiation of bills of exchange, accepted by the accepting houses, to which we later refer.

One more transformation of the City needs to be mentioned since it put an indelible stamp on procedures even as they are today. Towards the end of the seventeenth century, the East India Company started to import coffee into the country and coffee drinking became the fashion. As a result, numerous coffee houses started up in the City – and they became the meeting places for men of the City. There they traded in a variety of commodities and services and, for example, in the house of one, Lloyd, insurances of marine risks were transacted – the precursor of Lloyd's of London, now in Lime Street – and, in the house of another, shares were exchanged and thus The Stock Exchange was born. The messengers of Lloyd's of London and of The Stock Exchange are, to this day, called "waiters" to remind us of the usage made of the coffee houses and their staff.

It was not until the middle of the eighteenth century that the old City walls were largely pulled down and the City gates removed; but the removal of those restrictive barriers has not, in fact, resulted in much of an "outflow" of traditional "City" business to new sites.

So we come to the nineteenth and twentieth centuries in which the accepting houses started to operate in the City, and elsewhere, and gradually – in some cases rapidly – grew to their present eminence in the world of banking.

More recently, however, the accepting houses have met with increasing competition from the joint-stock or "clearing" banks and this chapter would be incomplete without a brief mention of their development. They are so named because of their common clearing system for the transfer of credit.

From the seventeenth century onwards most main towns in the United Kingdom had at least one private bank, and sometimes more, usually owned and managed by families, which served the domestic banking requirements of individuals and merchants in the area. Clearly, in conditions of slow and inefficient means of communication and travel, those banking relationships were adequate; but as travel became easier and the movement of people and of goods around the country became an everyday matter, a need for a broader-based, intercommunicating, banking system arose. To meet this requirement, a number of leading private banks began to operate together on a wider basis. That development led, in the nineteenth century, to the absorption of most of the country banking system by the bigger London and provincial banks, which itself led to further mergers and aggregations to achieve economies of size and more complete coverage of the whole country. The five remaining English clearing banks and their affiliates in Scotland and Northern Ireland now wield considerable influence but only in comparatively recent times have they developed overseas links and set up subsidiary banking activities in an endeavour to attract the type of business historically carried out by the accepting houses – in one case a clearing bank having purchased the whole share capital of an accepting house. Indeed each of the major clearing banks now has its merchant banking subsidiary, although the effect of operating under the umbrella of a powerful clearing house parent and the differing histories of most of these subsidiaries have tended to produce a type of merchant bank somewhat different from the rest of the accepting houses.

In addition to the competition between domestic U.K. banks, there are, as well as the consortium banks, some 380 overseas banks represented in London through branches or subsidiaries which compete for the available banking business. The Bank of England applies an "open door" policy to the establishment of foreign banks in England, and its flexible approach and the attractions of London as a financial centre have brought to London, especially since 1968, an inflow of foreign banks which compete with the merchant banks in all their fields of business.

2

THE MERCHANT BANKS: A PROBLEM OF DEFINITION

Humpty Dumpty in *Alice through the Looking Glass*, when asked by Alice how he could say that the word "glory" meant a "nice knockdown argument", said "It means just what I choose it to mean"! Those who have spent their working lives in merchant banking have no need to imitate Humpty Dumpty: they know what "merchant banking" means and who the genuine "merchant bankers" are. They do not follow the path trodden by some financial scribes and politicians in recent years who, although they may have glimpsed the truth, have deliberately by-passed it and, in the way of Humpty Dumpty, have chosen to use the words to mean anything – even if a little unsavoury – that they wished to make them mean. In so doing they have confused the traditional, old-established houses – those that have been described as the Davids of the City, in the sense that their capital and resources are small in comparison with those of the big commercial banks, but who exercise a Goliath's strength and wield a surprising influence – with the new kind of so-called merchant banks which fattened through the lush years of excessive money supply, only to starve, and in some cases die, in the leaner months that followed.

Although much has been written about the City of London itself, there remains great ignorance of its activities and, regrettably, some mistrust of its purpose and methods in the performance of its function as the heart of the financial bloodstream of the country. It would be foolish to pretend that sharp practice could not be found within the so-called "square mile", but it is right to say that those institutions which operate in

8

the centre of its financial sector, among which are numbered the accepting houses, have always maintained (and at all times will have to maintain) a strict code of business ethics and morality – otherwise they could not succeed in a nationally and internationally competitive environment in which "my word is my bond" is the behavioural keynote. This point will be re-emphasised in later chapters and is especially true for the accepting houses for reasons that will be explained.

This book, then, is about the old-established houses, how they started, how they grew, where they stand today – and, perhaps, how they will look in the future.

An Attempted Definition of Merchant Banking

The so-called merchant banks in London are now seldom merchants and by no means always bankers; the title is often misused as a generic description of businesses that operate in the financial sector, whether they perform pure banking services, or merchanting services, or not.

In the past there was nothing to prevent any business erecting a brass plaque on its premises on which it was described as a "merchant bank". However, since the passing of the *Banking Act, 1979* no person may describe his business as a bank or himself as a banker unless the business is included in the Bank of England's List of Recognised Banks. All the accepting houses are Recognised Banks. A number of institutions which formerly might have been described as merchant banks (and which the general public might still so describe) are in fact in the different category of licensed deposit-taking institutions (*i.e.* licensed under the *Banking Act*); and other businesses which might likewise have been loosely described as merchant banks (particularly those conducting no substantial banking business) have no standing at all under the Act.

It is indeed difficult to find clear definitions in existing literature; partly because the books already on the library shelves tend to be either historical novels or written by specialists on particular subjects, "talking shop" (as it were) to other practitioners in a specialist field; and partly because the pattern of the business of a merchant bank, as if seen through a kaleidoscope, is constantly changing and is not susceptible of an easy definition. Indeed, perhaps because of this, the difficulties of definition feed and multiply on themselves. But it is possible to "stop the clock" for the purposes of this book and provide a description, not only of what the old-established houses did do and still do, but also, by deduction, of what they do not do. For this purpose this book will be concerned only with the members of the Accepting Houses Committee (listed in Appendix A). This is a relatively small group – though not as small a group, in number of members, as, for example, the clearing banks or the discount houses; nor is it a "closed shop". But it is a group of specialists, of which the late Sir Edward J. Reid, Bt., himself the Chairman of the Accepting Houses Committee from 1946 until 1966, wrote:

An Accepting House is a firm or company, an important part of whose business consists of accepting Bills of Exchange to provide short-term finance for the trade of others. We have in the past been described as merchant banks and this description is historically correct as we, or most of us, started as merchants trading on our own account and the business gradually developed into a mercantile bank. The term "Accepting House" is, however, a more accurate description.

But that is a narrow definition which readers will find expanded upon in later paragraphs.

One further quotation, this from the Report of the Committee on the Working of the Monetary System (Radcliffe Report, 1959), will serve to underline the high measure of responsibility and reputation enjoyed by the accepting houses, which they jealously guard at all levels of employment:

These firms are nearly all companies, including some public companies, but all of them retain a strong element of their traditional ownership and management by families, some of whose names have stood high in world finance for a century or more.

To indicate another aspect of the problem of attempting a definition, there are 55 members of the Issuing Houses Association (listed in Appendix B), very many of which are generally referred to as merchant banks. These 56 include the 16 accepting houses; some of the others are also bankers or investment bankers, but many are neither.

The merchant banks, when acting in their role as issuing houses, are principally concerned in providing corporate finance services (*i.e.* advising companies, partnerships, or government or semi-government organisations and agencies on their financial requirements), including the advising of parties involved on either side of a take-over bid and in mergers. Strictly in that role, they do no banking business.

The accepting houses in particular – many, but certainly not all, of the other so-called "merchant banks" specialise in non-banking activities – provide all manner of financial services, which are more precisely described in following chapters, and the range of these services reflects the growing complexity of international business. Their activities were originally, and still are, intimately connected with foreign trade and with the international movement of goods and services, but the nature of their business, once often that of the merchant venturer and, therefore, concerned primarily with merchanting for their own account, has changed. This change occurred after the Second World War, as much as in the decades before it: but the arranging and financing of foreign trade is still an important function of an accepting house.

However, banks' customers do not have single financial problems for which single solutions are needed: they have a complex of interrelated problems to which there may be a number of answers – and the accepting house concerned, as adviser, must know all the possible answers and must recommend the combination that is appropriate. Such a combination of services includes advice on methods of funding and raising long-term capital, not only in London but also in world capital markets; the receiving of deposits and the making or arranging of loans – short term (whether in cash or by way of acceptance credit) and medium term; the issuing and the handling of certificates of deposit (sterling or foreign currency); the management of institutional and private investment portfolios; the handling of foreign exchange; the provision of insurance broking facilities; and advising and procuring advice on a wide range of financial and finance-related matters.

The accepting houses' services are by no means confined to London. In the next chapter we shall refer to the origins of some of the houses. Perhaps now – even more than in earlier days – the accepting houses have their associates, correspondents and subsidiaries around the world in an ever-widening circle, and their names on documents are as well recognised and trusted in distant lands as they are in London.

3

THE MERCHANT VENTURER

The concept of the merchant venturer was the starting-point for many of the accepting houses. Some, it is true, had their beginnings as a result of more positive leanings towards banking and finance, but all were established or eventually attracted to operate in London, where liberal surroundings beckoned them.

It does not take much imagination to appreciate the problems that the accepting houses met and had to overcome. The past two centuries are packed with factors that formed a backcloth for difficult trading conditions in which only the tenacious and the skilled could survive. To name but a few: revolutions – industrial, commercial, social and political; wars – continental and intercontinental, Napoleonic and others, leading up to the two world wars of our century; recession; and inflation.

The merchant venturer built his success on a number of special characteristics in his make-up. Perhaps the most important were:

(a) *Integrity* – a determination to build and then to protect his good name; his determination to ensure that he always lives up to the belief that his word is as good as his bond, not only at home but also abroad, binding him as surely as the most carefully worded and legally executed legal contract.

(b) *Expertise* – the intangible, technical skill which derives from a mixture of tradition, experience and, most important of all, dedication, coupled with natural flair to distinguish between the good and the bad in matters of business.

(c) *Adaptability and imagination* – which condition a man's flexibility of outlook and approach to change.

(*d*) *Tenacity* – giving no quarter to defeat even in periods of extreme crisis and disaster to others. Certainly there have been defeats and temporary difficulties among the accepting houses, but the debts have been repaid and the businesses rebuilt.

Transition from Merchant Venturer to Accepting House

It is important to recognise how the merchant venturer made use of the qualities named to bring about his transition from being a merchant for his own account to being both that and a banker for merchants.

It has already been mentioned that, in their beginnings, many merchant bankers occupied themselves principally in overseas trade. Some used their own (or chartered) ships to convey manufactured goods from the then developed countries of Europe to, for example, the countries of North and South America and the Far East, where they sold them direct or through local agents, or, later, through their own offices in those countries, which were frequently managed by members of the merchant venturer's own family. With the proceeds, indigenous products were purchased, usually, in fact, in earliest days by direct barter, and shipped back to Europe.

From the beginning, while they were buying, shipping and selling for their own account, merchant bankers developed a network of overseas connections for whom they bought in Europe, subsequently selling products from overseas for account of the same parties.

Their overseas connections became – and often remained – their banking clients, who deposited with them the proceeds of the sale, in Europe, of their local products; thus, too, their overseas customers became investors in the United Kingdom and also invested in bonds and shares of other overseas countries, relying on the merchant bank to care for their investments, to collect their dividends and to finance their shipments, whether of manufactured goods inwards or indigenous raw materials outwards. Finance for shipments from the overseas country was usually arranged by the exporter drawing a bill of exchange on his merchant bank for an agreed proportion of the value of the cargo and by selling that bill of exchange (the bill on London) to a local banker at a discount. The local banker then forwarded the bill to his London agent who presented it, accompanied by the shipping documents, to the merchant banker, who would "accept" it as duly payable on a date stated and retain the shipping documents. The due date for payment of the bill – previously agreed with the shipper – would be decided upon to allow for the goods to be sold and the payment to be received before the merchant bank was required to pay the value of the bill. Thus the shipper received the main value for his shipment when the ship was loaded; the intermediate banker received interest, by way of discount on his purchase price for the bill in the first place, for the money he advanced; and the merchant banker charged his overseas client an acceptance commission for the privilege given to the client by way of an undertaking to accept the bill on first presentation in London.

It was in this way the accepting houses built up their original overseas banking connections and also the way in which they built up their reputation for fair and honest dealing.

Of course, so long as the values of the goods purchased and sold were in balance, no need for international transfers of funds existed, but the merchant bankers tended, later, to alter the pattern of their business to such an extent that their exports and imports were brought into a state of imbalance, thus creating a need for international movements of credit; and so, as business developed, London became the centre of world trade and sterling the world's trading currency – even for goods that, in fact, never touched England's shores. This development led to a special use of the bill of exchange, whereby credit was transferred from one overseas country to another by means of a bill drawn in sterling on a London banker, the bill being saleable by the beneficiary either to a local banker or, less expensively, to another local merchant who was buying goods in London and needed the sterling to pay for them.

Use of the bill of exchange was later recognised and expressed in the *Bills of Exchange Act*, 1882 in the following words:

A Bill of Exchange is an unconditional order in writing, addressed by one person to another, signed by the person giving it, requiring the person to whom it is addressed to pay on demand or at a fixed or determinable future time a sum certain in money to or to the order of a specified person or to bearer.

But, of course, even the legal definition, when introduced, was of no value to the owner of the bill unless he could absolutely rely upon the drawee to pay on the agreed date. Many London merchants did possess good reputations and bills were freely and fearlessly drawn on them; but there were evident dangers to the holders of a bill drawn on a less creditworthy name and so the habit grew up of "borrowing" the name of a fully trusted London merchant and paying the latter a commission for his acceptance and due payment of the bill – thus the title "accepting house".

Further Sophistication in the Use of the Sterling Bill of Exchange

So these international merchant bankers – the accepting houses of today – began their gradual change into bankers for international merchants, as well as for international trade, and enlarged their spheres of operation and of influence by accepting bills of exchange drawn on them by the sellers of goods of which they might not themselves be the purchasers – bills of exchange drawn to finance international trading transactions to which they themselves were not necessarily a party.

In the nineteenth century, the bill on London, which was the very essence of the accepting house, became the main instrument of payment for all goods and produce moving internationally. A bill drawn on one of the accepting houses, under authority of a letter of credit issued to the drawer by the accepting house, was not only the preferred means of international payment but also frequently preferable to local currency, although the bill itself was almost invariably expressed in sterling – settlements between Philadelphia and Boston, for example, until well after the Civil War, were most easily carried out by sterling bills on London.

With a merchant's understanding of mercantile problems, the accepting houses made this business simple for a seller of goods, and for the buyer, by creating a variation of the letter of credit (in fact, an old banking instrument which, in its simple form, was used by the Greeks way back in the fourth century B.C.). For their special purpose the nineteenth-century merchant bankers called it a documentary letter of credit (now simply called a "documentary credit") and introduced a condition into it. At the request of the actual buyer of the goods, and in accordance with his detailed instructions, they authorised the seller to draw his bill of exchange on them and undertook to accept it on first presentation *provided that* it was accompanied by specified shipping and other documents relating to the goods. The seller could be perfectly sure that he would be drawing a bill of exchange which was "as safe as the Bank of England" and that, as a result, he could at once sell it to someone else and thus receive its present value in hard cash immediately. The buyer could still get his period of credit, making his own arrangements with the merchant banker regarding release of the goods, either on providing funds in cover or in anticipation of so doing. The merchant banker, charging a commission for this use of his name, had to meet the accepted bill of exchange at maturity for the honour of that name even if the buyer had failed to carry out his part of the bargain, *i.e.* to provide funds in cover at the latest at the date of maturity.

Thus, knowledge, tradition, the good name of specialist houses and the international information to which they had access via agents or correspondents overseas were used to extend credit facilities to people in all parts of the world.

4

THE NEXT PHASE: SPECIALISATION

Overseas Loans

Arising out of their overseas connections thus developed, the accepting houses grew to be recognised as bankers, and as consultants on banking and investment matters, not only by their U.K. and overseas private customers, but also by overseas local and central governments. They were recognised as having special knowledge of the areas in which they operated, and London became the principal financial centre where overseas borrowers could raise loans by bond issues. Hence, as many "underdeveloped" overseas countries began their long trek towards "development", their local and central governments came to take financial advice from the London accepting houses and to raise loans in Europe and elsewhere, employing the accepting houses, as their agents, to issue the loans and to service them on their behalf.

The zenith of the political influence of the accepting houses was probably reached during the Napoleonic Wars and the two decades which followed, when the foreign policies of the Great Powers depended heavily on the international financial arrangements which only the merchant bankers could provide. But simultaneously with these operations and subsequently up until 1914 the accepting houses, through the raising of loans, financed the infrastructure required to market, world-wide, the manufactured goods which were emerging from the Industrial Revolution on the one hand and, on the other hand, the purchase of food and raw materials which were increasingly being

17

produced in faraway lands to meet the demands of the industrial countries.

The canal age was being supplanted by the railway, the clipper ship by the steamship. Both in the United States and in Canada, railways which linked Atlantic to Pacific, the Trans-Siberian Railway in Asia, the railways of Europe, South America and the Indian sub-continent, all looked to the accepting houses for finance. Waterworks, docks and other public works of every kind around the world were financed by loans, raised on the London market, of funds subscribed predominantly by the increasingly rich British merchants and manufacturers, but in large part, too, from foreign investors who regarded sterling as the most trustworthy currency for investment.

So it was that an international market in international loans grew up in the City of London, only to be crippled by the aftermath of war and resulting exchange control. In the meantime, however, many trading benefits accrued to the U.K. banking and industrial sectors from the initiative displayed in these matters by the accepting houses – some of which also took a principal role in underwriting and marketing British Government debt, prior to the appointment of the Bank of England to perform that function.

Sterling as a World Currency

As an adjunct to their paramount position in the overseas banking field, the accepting houses held deposits not only for their overseas customers and associates but also for foreign governments. Thus the growth of the accepting houses was inextricably interwoven into the history of sterling as a world currency and this factor, together with the growth of the financial reserves of Britain's colonial empire which were deposited in London, and with the financial reserves of many other countries who chose, as the highest-degree security, to hold their reserves in sterling, provided London with the then unchallengeable role of provider of world-wide development finance and the currency in which virtually all international indebtedness was settled.

Simultaneously with their development of business in bills of exchange, the accepting houses became the central market for that type of financial instrument, which itself became accepted as a form of international currency. Indeed, such was the predominance of sterling as a currency, in the form of bills on London, for the settlement of international indebtedness, that on the outbreak of the First World War in 1914, when bank rate was raised to 10%, the American money market, together with other financial markets around the world, was thrown into a state of near collapse.

Domestic Activities

Short-term Lending: Acceptance Credits

In 1931 the Macmillan Committee reported as follows:

In connection with short-term credit, all concerned would benefit by a more extended use of commercial bills.

This led to the adaptation by the accepting houses of their acceptance facilities so as to result in their greater use by the home trade (in the form of acceptance credits) to finance short-term requirements such, for example, as the financing of raw materials in bonded warehouses pending processing, manufacture and sale. With interest rates low and an adequate supply of money in the discount market for the purchase of bills of exchange, it often proves cheaper for industry to borrow on a short-term basis in this way, extending the borrowing at maturity by drawing a "renewal" bill of exchange, the discount of which provides funds to meet the maturing one.

It must be appreciated and emphasised, however, that the purposes for which it was, and still is, permissible to use acceptance credits are more restricted than those applying to bank overdrafts. A bill of exchange, to be acceptable for rediscount by the Bank of England as the lender of last resort to the banking sector, must be related to a self-liquidating current transaction that will be completed within the term ("tenor") of the bill – and that should not normally exceed three to four months. Furthermore, bill finance can be appropriate for short-term borrowing only if both the drawer and the acceptor are satisfied that a ready market exists for the bill in the money market within the City of London; and that the discount market, which is normally the first buyer, will buy the bill at the finest discount rate because it can, if necessary, tender it to the Bank of England as first-class security for its own required borrowings from the central bank.

Of course, the accepting house must pay the bill at maturity, whether or not cash cover has been provided to it by its customer. However inconceivable, it is worth saying that the money market system in the City would be thrown into confusion if an accepting house failed to honour its own acceptance at maturity – and that has never happened.

(There will be further reference, in Chapters 5 and 12, to the internal and external disciplines brought to bear on the acceptance and other business of an accepting house so as to ensure its liquidity and solvency.)

Other Short- to Medium-term Lending

The accepting houses do not benefit from the great volume of interest-free current accounts which are principally held by the clearing banks, largely from their private banking clients. The accepting houses do, none the less, make short-term direct loan facilities available to their customers on terms that compare with those offered by the clearing banks and they finance these by "buying" deposits from their customers and other banks – whether in sterling or in foreign currencies.

Thus, it may be claimed that the accepting houses compete directly with other banks in the provision of loan facilities and so offer to their clients alternative sources of short-term finance – fixed advance or acceptance credit – which can be used according to which is the cheaper and/or more appropriate for the particular transaction. The versatility of the accepting houses in these fields is unmatched.

At the longer end of their short- to medium-term lending activities, the accepting houses were largely instrumental in developing the provision of finance for high-value export contracts based upon a guarantee of the overseas buyer granted by the Export Credits Guarantee Department of the Secretary of State for Trade (E.C.G.D.). Some years ago, operating overseas in a manner similar to that of their ancestors, the accepting houses reinforced their studies of the requirements of overseas buyers for U.K. manufactured goods and jointly with the manufacturers themselves, and supported by the E.C.G.D., fostered a high percentage of U.K. exports on credit terms. In later times other agencies, particularly the clearing banks, have played an increasing part in this type of business, but the accepting houses are still leading the field in arranging large export contracts for U.K. suppliers, thus again showing their adaptability and imagination in business development. (*See also* Chapter 7.)

Corporate Finance

Before the Second World War the accepting houses acted as

issuers of bonds and managers of loans for overseas – and, later, for domestic – borrowers in an important way. After the Second World War they developed their corporate finance capability and have taken the leading role in raising permanent and long-term finance within the United Kingdom and, for United Kingdom borrowers, overseas. The increasing need for industry to regroup into larger, more cost-effective units and other financial pressures and distortions brought about the take-over and merger situations of which much has been heard in recent years. The accepting houses, and the other issuing houses, are the leaders in the provision of expert advice to both (or all) parties in these situations, as well as in the field of new issues and other financial transactions where regrouping and reconstruction is necessary to the continued success of the organisation concerned. (*See* Chapter 8 for more information on these activities.)

International Capital Market

Following on the development of the international money market, an important new international capital market has developed since 1963. Although it has spread during this period right across the world, encompassing the principal European capitals as well as Tokyo, Singapore and other cities, London is still its centre. The accepting houses have made a significant contribution to the pioneering and expansion of this market and numerous British companies and public institutions have had access to it.

Bond issues in the international capital market are made in all the major convertible currencies. The bonds are purchased, for the most part, by investors in countries outside that of the currency in which the loan is denominated. The most important segment of this market has been developed in issues in U.S. dollars, subscribed by non-residents of the United States. Very large amounts have, however, also been raised in Deutschmarks, Dutch guilders, sterling, Swiss, French, Belgian and Luxembourg francs, Japanese yen and certain Arabian currencies, as well as in combinations of currencies such as sterling/Deutschmarks, European Units of Account, European Currency Units and Special Drawing Rights.

The total volume of all issues has now reached over U.S. $160 billion (or equivalent in other currencies), the annual rate of issue having grown from a little over U.S. $1 billion in 1965 to more than U.S. $24 billion in 1981.

In first helping to create these new forms of business, and then in building them up, the accepting houses can claim to have sponsored the development of the new international money market (the Eurocurrency market) and the international capital market (the Eurobond market), to the great advantage of the United Kingdom's balance of payments, and the financing of world trade.

The international capital market is further described in Chapter 9.

Investment Advisory Services

The Radcliffe Report said:

Investment Advisory Service is something in which the accepting houses specialise to a far greater extent than other financial institutions . . . they manage, or have advisory influence upon the management of, private investments amounting to hundreds of millions of pounds.

This remains true today, although the figures, now thousands of millions of pounds worth, are much higher than in 1959 when the Radcliffe Report was published.

The accepting houses cover the entire sphere of investment advice: they advise private and institutional clients; they manage pension funds, investment trusts and unit trusts. As a separate allied function, they play an important part in the underwriting of new issues.

It is sometimes questioned whether the same house that is advising, for example, an industrial company on reconstruction or on a merger or take-over should be entitled also to be advising clients on investment portfolios which may, fortuitously, include investments in that client company. The Panel on Take-overs and Mergers investigated this subject in depth in 1969–70. Extracts from its comments, made in its Annual Report of the latter year, are given in Appendix C. This interesting Report is noteworthy for the evaluation it makes of the high standard of integrity maintained by the accepting houses.

The investment advisory role of the accepting houses is further described in Chapter 13.

Ancillary Activities

The development of their businesses over the decades has resulted in accepting houses withdrawing from some fields of activity which they have found no longer remunerative or complementary to their main business and entering into other fields of activity in which they see a profitable opening. There is no stereotype of an accepting house to which all conform. All are involved in the activities described in Chapters 6–9, 11–13 and 15. Only some are involved in the activities described in Chapters 10, 14, 16 and 17.

The first edition of this book contained chapters on trading in commodities and on factoring. Commodity trading was seen as the natural successor to the old merchanting activities of the merchant banks and in 1976, when the first edition was published, there were at least two accepting house groups still directly involved in commodity trading. Writing now, it would be timely to say that the main connection of the accepting houses with commodity trading is as bankers to those directly involved as traders. Likewise, the present members of the Accepting Houses Committee are no longer directly involved in the business of the factoring of debts.

Various members of the Accepting Houses Committee (or subsidiaries or associated companies within their groups) provide a number of other financial services – for example, as company registrars, as professional executors and trustees or as advisers in the provision of employee benefits for corporate and other clients. Some, as part of their banking activities, specialise in putting together financial packages to finance the production of a film or the building or purchase of a ship. The accepting houses vary, *inter se*, in the nature, as in the size, of their businesses.

5

LIQUIDITY AND THE ROLE OF THE ACCEPTING HOUSES COMMITTEE

Liquidity

The following is extracted from the Parker Bank Rate Tribunal's Report of 1957:

The nature of the business of the Accepting Houses requires them to keep a higher liquidity ratio than the ordinary joint-stock banks. Large sums are deposited with them by their clients, many of whom are foreign depositors, and pressure on the pound leads to withdrawal of deposits. It is normal for them to maintain a ratio in excess of 50% of cash, call money and Treasury and Bank bills to their total deposits.

This is an important point and, indeed, one which cannot be overstressed in relation to the whole of the banking business of an accepting house; but, in particular, to its acceptance business, as emphasised in the following extract from the 1959 Radcliffe Report:

A bill of exchange accepted by one of the accepting houses is, if it has one other British name on it, "eligible paper" at the Bank of England, and has therefore the highest degree of liquidity, shared only by Treasury Bills and short-dated Government bonds. Having this maximum of liquidity and the complete assurance of payment (on which of course the liquidity depends), it commands the lowest rate of discount available for any non-Government paper. An accepting house thus, when accepting a bill, confers on the drawer of the bill (and on anyone who discounts it for him) the certainty of being able to get sterling in exchange for it from a bank or discount house in London, at the least possible sacrifice in discount. In order to retain this power, an accepting house has continually to satisfy the Bank of England that it has adequate capital and adequate liquidity and that it is maintaining its reputation generally.

The accepting houses, being "recognised" British banks, are required to comply with the Bank of England's guidelines which have been established with regard to capital adequacy, liquidity and foreign exchange exposure. However, the Bank's control is also on a more personal level and goes well beyond a requirement to fill in standard forms. Indeed, each of the accepting houses is required, three or four times a year, to report personally through its Chairman or Senior Banking Director to the Bank of England on its balance sheet and profit and loss items, and to keep in touch with the Bank regularly throughout each year to draw to the Bank's attention, and to give an explanation for, any significant changes in its financial position or in its pattern of business.

The Accepting Houses Committee

It was not until 1914, at the beginning of the First World War, that the Accepting Houses Committee was formed. The original purpose was to meet, together, the crisis of illiquidity which hit some of the merchant banks as a result of the non-payment of debts owing to them from Germany and her allies: this crisis demanded difficult negotiations with the Bank of England and Government and a measure of financial assistance.

At the end of the war, the Bank, finding this negotiating committee a useful means of communication with an important part of the London banking sector, proposed that the Committee should remain in existence, to provide a forum for discussion of matters of mutual interest and as a negotiating body with which also to discuss banking and legislative matters.

The Accepting Houses Committee has no written regulations or rules, and remains in being, on an informal basis, for these purposes alone. At the time of writing it has a Director-General, a Secretary, an Assistant Secretary and four members of staff. The two Secretaries act also as Secretaries to the Issuing Houses Association.

On signature by the British Government in 1972 of the Deed of Accession to the European Economic Community, the British Bankers' Association was reconstituted (*inter alia*) to incorporate the accepting houses for the first time. The accepting houses are now represented on the General Council and on the Executive Committee of the British Bankers' Association, which plays an important role in the Fédération Bancaire. The Fédération Bancaire is the forum of the principal banking associations of the E.E.C. countries and represents their banking interests to the E.E.C. Commission.

The accepting houses are represented on the City Liaison Committee; on the Council for the Securities Industry; on the Committee on Invisible Exports; and on the Confederation of British Industry. They subscribe to the City Code on Take-overs and Mergers, having played a part in the original preparation and subsequent amendments to that code, and they provide a representative at all formal meetings of the Panel. They also play a part in a number of other committees within the City of London and outside it and, through their Chairmen, have direct access to the Governor of the Bank of England and, through him, to Government departments.

The Committee is not, as is sometimes thought, a closed shop. New members, since the Second World War, were elected in 1946 (Antony Gibbs & Sons Limited); 1952 (Arbuthnot Latham & Co. Limited); 1969 (Rea Brothers p.l.c.); 1973 (Singer & Friedlander Limited); and 1980 (Robert Fleming & Co. Limited). Over the years some companies have ceased to be members of the Committee, either as a consequence of mergers or because they were no longer qualified for membership.

The Accepting Houses Committee is an association of British banks and it has been regarded as a criterion for membership that the Committee should be satisfied as to the ownership of a house's share capital and that the house should enjoy day-to-day independence of management. The principal other qualifications for membership are that a house has a first-class reputation, does a meaningful acceptance business and that its acceptances are discountable at the finest Bank bill rate: in other words – that it satisfies the other members of the Committee and the Bank of England that, having for some time enjoyed full banking status, it has a first-class reputation and *that it intends to make its principal business that of a bank run on prudent lines with the interests of its depositors, as well as its shareholders, at heart*. It must also satisfy the Committee of its determination to perform the other functions of an accepting house as indicated in previous chapters.

The Accepting Houses Committee is part of the self-regulatory mechanism of the City. Believing that it is possible for those who work in the City to evolve rules of conduct far more expeditiously than Parliament can enact a statute, and to make effective principles of behaviour which do not lend themselves to enshrinement in a statute, the Committee supported the establishment of the Panel on Take-overs and Mergers and the Council for the Securities Industry.

The accepting houses were in origin all family-owned and controlled partnerships. Today they are all limited companies and there is a Stock Exchange Listing of the ordinary share capital of all but three of them (or of their holding companies). Within a number of them there is still a large or preponderant family influence. A number are owned within large industrial holding groups of companies, but the majority are part (often the major part) of groups whose activities consist only of banking and ancillary financial activities.

As the Preface of this book explains, the chapters that follow have been written by experts in their own field and provide valuable guides to elements of the work of an accepting house which have already been mentioned in Chapter 4.

PART TWO

PROVISION OF FINANCE

6

SHORT-TERM FINANCE

Accepting houses are, no doubt, particularly associated in the public mind with their most widely publicised activities, namely their corporate advisory services. Nevertheless, it is the more straightforward business of commercial banking which represents their single most important area of activity. It is probable that the majority of the accepting houses employ a greater proportion of their staff in this field than in any other and derive a greater proportion of their profits from it.

It is important to emphasise the wholesale nature of the accepting houses' business. They do not usually seek to attract accounts or business from the general public (although some do); such business necessitates the employment of larger numbers of staff. The accepting houses are not normally interested in a deposit of less than £25,000 or a loan of less than £50,000, the minimum unit used in the London money market (although some are). But the wholesale approach goes further: for their clientèle of industrial and commercial companies, banks, institutions, Government agencies and a few wealthy private individuals, the accepting houses usually only attempt to handle certain specialised services. Because of this, it is rare for an accepting house to be regarded by any major enterprise as its main banker.

Accepting houses are also very centralised. While some of the larger ones have branches or subsidiaries overseas, in the Channel Islands, the Isle of Man and in the provinces, these offices do not usually handle large amounts of business themselves. They find new business for the bank and anything important is referred back to be dealt with at Head Office. In the banking field this system has the great advantages that decisions are taken at a high level and that a strong element of control can be maintained.

The majority of this banking business is conducted at short term. It is one of the banker's golden rules that he must preserve his liquidity and there is not a great deal of money which is deposited in banks for more than one year. But in addition to avoiding the sin of "borrowing short and lending long", the banker must also look to the durability of his assets. This is the fundamental reason why the acceptance credit remains the classic form of banking business for the accepting houses who thence derived their generic name, although the proportion of their assets in this form has varied in recent years with the changes in exchange control and customer demand for a wider range of financing alternatives.

Acceptance Finance

The acceptance credit had its origins in the days (as explained in earlier chapters) when the present merchant banks were primarily merchants themselves. Smaller traders would ask the larger merchants in the City to add their name to trade bills in order to make them readily acceptable to foreign sellers of goods or to bankers abroad and at home. Today, this adding of their name has become for the accepting houses a regular and more precise form of financial assistance to their customers. The customer draws a bill on his accepting house, which accepts it and, as its acceptor, becomes primarily responsible for its payment at maturity. Such a bill is then immediately saleable, at a discount which reflects the cost of money until the maturity of the bill, when it will be paid by the acceptor at its face value. In practice, the bill is normally discounted and the accepting house can arrange the discounting on behalf of its customer with the London discount market, a group of 12 institutions – the discount houses (*see* Appendix D) – whose function it is to act as a buffer for the supply of money between the Bank of England and the banking system.

In its purest form, the acceptance credit is used for the finance of trade, often international trade. The provision of this form of credit should always involve the bridging of a gap and therefore be self-liquidating; and with an international trade transaction, not only is a gap of time (between the seller requiring to be paid for his goods and the buyer selling them for cash in his own market) being bridged, but also gaps between a producer and consumer, between a supplier and a buyer and between one country and another, probably involving two different currencies. All accepted bills should reflect these gaps: they should be drawn at arm's length (*i.e.* not contrived between one party and another under his control – the market requires to see "two good names" on a bill); they should cover a genuine transaction concerned with the current movement or production of goods (and not be used to substitute for permanent capital); and, where the bill is drawn by a foreign customer, the underlying transaction must involve international trade and, in consequence, a conversion of currency.

The mechanism for mobilising a bill for acceptance is quite straightforward. Take the case of a British company exporting goods to the United States: as soon as it makes the shipment, the British company would draw a bill on its accepting house to mature at the time the payment is due from its American customer. The accepting house would accept the bill and arrange its discounting, paying the proceeds, after deducting the financial charges (the cost of discounting and the house's accepting commission), to the British company. The bill would be met at maturity by means of the American buyer making payment direct to the accepting house for account of the British supplier. If for any reason the payment had not arrived by the due date (for example if the American buyer had gone bankrupt or if the payment had been transmitted astray by his bank), then the British company would be liable under the facility to pay the full value of the bill to the accepting house, who would have met the bill at maturity by paying the face value to its holder (probably, but not necessarily, a discount house).

If the goods had been invoiced in a foreign currency, say, in U.S. dollars, the British company could draw a bill denominated in dollars, the bill could be accepted for the sterling equivalent of the U.S. dollar face value and the discount proceeds paid to the British company in sterling or the transaction could remain in dollars with the British company receiving the discount proceeds in that currency. A third possibility is for the British company to draw in sterling and arrange with the accepting house to sell the dollars receivable forward against sterling for the date on which the payment is due. In each case the accepting house should receive a payment in U.S. dollars from the American buyer.

Nowadays, acceptance credits are also widely used by British companies as a means of raising credit for domestic purposes. For most large and many medium-sized companies, they constitute the second most important source of short-term finance after bank overdrafts (which are of course mainly provided by clearing banks, the accepting houses not possessing the same range of relatively low-cost balances deriving from small current and savings accounts). Normally the company will negotiate a facility for a stipulated amount with its accepting house which is then made available, either "until further notice" like an overdraft or for a certain fixed period, in which case the customer pays a "commitment commission" in order to compensate the house for the earmarking of some of its resources to that customer. The facility is normally available on a "revolving" basis, that is to say that, upon the maturity of a bill, a new bill may be drawn against fresh business, leaving the customer to pay only the finance charges on the new bill rather than the face value of the maturing bill. Quite often, companies involved in a seasonal business may require the facility only at certain times of the year and acceptance credits are particularly well suited to such requirements.

In the case of larger companies requiring greater facilities than the accepting house would wish to provide by itself, it is usual for the house concerned to invite other banks to form a "syndicate" by taking participations in the facility. In this case, the customer will make drawings on the several banks participating in the facility, in proportion to their shares of participation. Where large drawings are concerned, the customer will be asked to split up the amount he requires to draw into a number of bills, so that the face value of each bill is not more than £250,000 or possibly £500,000; this is for the convenience of the discount market, whose practice it is to deposit bank bills (and other securities) as collateral security for the deposits they accept from the banking system.

Given their trading background which often involves a self-liquidating transaction, acceptance credits are usually granted on an unsecured basis, unlike overdrafts for which the bank often has some sort of charge over the company's assets. It is common, however, for an accepting house granting an acceptance credit to incorporate a "negative pledge" clause in the arrangements, under which the company (the customer) undertakes not to pledge its assets elsewhere without the house's consent, thus affording the house some protection. Bills are drawn most frequently for a period of 90 days, but circumstances can vary this period; the maximum period normally allowed by the Bank of England and by the discount market is 180 days and bills seldom have a "tenor" of less than 60 days. The commission which accepting houses currently charge for accepting bills ranges from ¼% per annum or even lower for bills guaranteed by the United Kingdom Government, to 1% per annum or more in the case of less gilt-edged customers, but the commission is liable to fluctuation in the light of changes in competition and perceived risk. The commission charged on a three-month bill is, of course, one-quarter of the per annum charge.

Bills should always bear a "clausing", showing the transaction against which they are drawn. In times of stringency the discount market is likely to draw a distinction between bills drawn against trade and those drawn as finance paper, *e.g.* to finance hire purchase receivables. The Bank of England will also check on bills from time to time to see that the quality of bills in the market is being maintained. They are particularly concerned with the quality of eligible bills, which are bills accepted by the banks on the Bank of England's "eligible list", which includes all the accepting houses. An eligible bill must be drawn by a commercial body (not a bank) for a period of six months or less to finance trade between any two countries or domestic trade in the United Kingdom.

The accepting houses still account for 25% of all the acceptance business done, although their position is under attack by the foreign banks (who have recently invaded this field), as well as by the British clearing and overseas banks.

Short-term Advances

In addition to lending their name by way of accepting, the accepting houses also lend their money or more accurately – as with all banks – their depositors' money. Here again the international aspect of the accepting houses is clearly manifested: half of their commercial advances are to overseas borrowers and over 80% of these are made in foreign currencies. This major involvement in international business led to a substantial increase in the proportion of advances to acceptances when the United Kingdom had exchange control, but this has reversed to some extent since 1981 as foreign customers have been re-educated in the ways of the London acceptance market.

The growth in international business results from a wide spread of international connections and the general inability of capital markets outside North America to cater for the requirements of their domestic customers. This gap has been filled by the international money markets and London remains the most important centre in these markets, while banks in the City have enjoyed more freedom to operate in these markets than their counterparts in any other major international financial centre. While banks in other countries have had various controls imposed upon them from time to time by their central banks and regulatory authorities, banks in London have been permitted to finance almost any international business with deposits obtained from the Eurocurrency market. The City has not been slow to take advantage of this comparative freedom and the accepting houses have played an important part in the development of this business.

Their short-term lending is very varied, covering business which would not be suitable for bill finance, such as bridging loans and loans for very short periods or at notice, as well as competing with bills. Customers abroad are still often unwilling to draw bills because of the problem of sending them to London and, in addition, many countries impose costly stamp duties on bills of exchange.

Loans are normally made for a fixed period, but they can also be at call, at two days' notice or at seven days' notice if this suits the customer's requirements. Bankers normally classify as "short term" any finance not exceeding one year in duration; this classification is reflected both in the Eurocurrency market and in the London domestic market, in both of which deposits for more than a year (and sometimes for more than six months) are not easy to find. Borrowing facilities which permit the customer to borrow and repay periodically may be granted, as with acceptance credits. The main considerations for the bank, as always, are that the borrower should be creditworthy in his own right and that he should be able to demonstrate how the loan will be repaid. The bank may on occasion require security, and if asked to lend to a foreign subsidiary of an international company will probably require a guarantee or at least a letter of support or "comfort" from the parent company.

This lending activity, whether for trade or other purposes, today covers almost the entire world. Individual accepting houses have particular historical ties with or special strength in particular countries – most frequently with the industrialised nations of North America, Europe and the Far East. As a body they can claim to be closely involved in every important industry in every important country in the world. Always the pioneering spirit is there. Many times more often than their relative size would imply, they are covering new markets, making new contacts and suggesting new methods of reducing the cost of borrowing by exploiting a combination of inventiveness and technical skill.

Other Short-term Financial Services

The short-term assistance which the accepting houses give to industry and commerce is therefore based on their advances and acceptances. As has been observed earlier, most do not grant overdraft facilities to a great extent. The others have to, and do, compete in this field with the clearing banks, with their mass of relatively cheap money kept in a large number of accounts by the public. Such overdraft facilities as the houses do provide have to be rationed and are financed from their limited number of current accounts and from short-notice accounts which they seek to attract of a size sufficient to avoid their becoming too numerous and labour-intensive.

Another peripheral service which the accepting houses offer to British industry is that of money market loans for very short periods. Instead of making formal advances for fixed periods of six months or one year, the accepting houses may lend to certain companies for very short periods, often just one day and seldom more than a month. This business is done on an informal basis with a limited number of first-class companies, who borrow direct from the money market through the accepting houses to finance their day-to-day cash positions.

The accepting houses are also active in providing short-term finance indirectly to industry by negotiating bills of exchange or promissory notes drawn between third parties. They may either endorse them and discount them with the discount market or elsewhere or they may finance them themselves out of their own deposits. Occasionally an accepting house may also discount its own acceptances by "holding them in portfolio" if, for example, it can finance them more cheaply than the discount market or if it wishes to hold such bills for technical reasons.

Finally, these banks also carry out all the normal banking services that corporate customers might require. They issue guarantees on their behalf and are prepared to put up indemnities or bonds, normally against a counter-indemnity from the customer. They also, of course, issue documentary credits,

undertake documentary collections and act as confirming banks
for credits opened by banks abroad on behalf of foreign importers.
Although this "documentary" business is nowadays by no means
unique to the accepting houses, they nevertheless played an
important part in its development, particularly in the last century
before the larger banks had begun to deal with foreign business.

The documentary credit enables an exporter to be paid for his
merchandise upon his presenting a specified set of shipping
documents to the importer's bank; it thus plays a key part in
international trade, very often being the factor which decides a
seller to make the export in a situation which would otherwise be
uncertain. If the exporter is still uncertain of the bank issuing the
credit, he may require a bank that he does know to confirm it – and
London accepting houses still confirm many credits between
"third countries" as well as those in favour of British exporters.
Documentary collections are similar in that a bank is charged with
collecting cash against the handing over of certain specified
documents. In handling this documentary business, for imports,
exports and third-country trade, accepting houses are usually able
to give their customers a much quicker and more efficient service
than that obtainable from a large bank. The standard of individual
attention to a customer's affairs applies as much to the more
routine functions as it does to the most complex transactions.

7

MEDIUM-TERM FINANCE

Medium-term finance is not a precise concept, and there are many forms in which it can be made available. It is normally of two to seven years' term, and is applied to purposes other than working capital. But even this tentative outline of the nature of medium-term finance is unsatisfactory. Some capital market instruments, such as the seven-year loan notes common in U.S. markets and the seven-year dollar bonds issued in Eurocurrency markets, are undoubtedly of medium term. Equally, some bank lending – particularly abroad – has more of the characteristics of long-term funded debt than of medium-term bank credit. Neither can one invariably assume that medium-term finance should never be applied to working capital needs: it is possible to argue that any company has available to it, according to the nature of its business, a general portfolio of credit for the conduct of that business. The structure of a company's funding will affect – whether for better or for worse – its ability to get funds of any particular kind in the future. There are methods of financing which aim, among other things, to reduce the interdependence of various forms of finance. Such methods range from leasing (where the capital cost of an asset of which the business has sole use does not appear in the balance sheet) to project loans (where the security for a particular loan rests solely in specific assets and their earning power). A number of these financing alternatives are described in the succeeding pages.

The concept of medium-term finance is most conventionally associated with bank lending. Term loans – made by banks for a specified period of more than a year, and often repayable in equal instalments over the life of the loan – originated in the United States, and in most cases the interest rate was fixed for the life of the loan. As inflation slowly gathered pace in virtually all industrialised countries after the Second World War, the main attraction of such loans came to be the fixed rate of interest rather than the commitment by the bank to the lender. In the United Kingdom the clearing banks, which have usually taken a fairly cautious line on new forms of financing and which prefer to retain liquid portfolios, did not enter the business of providing medium-term finance for some time, and then usually at a floating interest rate linked to base rate. In recent years, however, the situation has changed and the four leading British clearing banks all now feature very near the top of the medium-term Eurocurrency lenders' league table. This business has elicited very different responses from the various accepting houses. Some take the view that participation in it is an essential part of their role, and have therefore attempted to expand their capital base to enable them to take on a good volume of business. Others have concluded that the uniqueness of an accepting house lies not in its financial muscle, but in its ability to orchestrate and arrange finance for its clients, and, where necessary, to develop new forms of finance to meet particular needs.

Domestic Currency Lending

Medium-term domestic currency lending is usually carried out under a facility letter, which sets out the terms that borrower and lender have agreed between each other. Such a letter will cover the sum to be lent, the method of determining the rate of interest, the schedule of drawdown and repayment, the security to be offered by the borrower and the circumstances under which the lender may withdraw his loan, among other, less important, details. Facility letters do not follow a standard form, but are the result of negotiation between the parties concerned and their advisers. If an accepting house does not wish to provide all the loan funds itself, it will arrange, with the permission of the borrower, a syndicate of banks, whose members will together provide the sum required. The accepting house or other bank which arranged the syndicate will normally become the manager, monitoring the progress of the borrower to ensure that he does not go into default on the terms and conditions of the loan, and acting as paying agent for interest and capital repayments.

Commercial banks are not the only financial institutions prepared to lend money on a medium-term basis. A few insurance companies have made such loans, but there does not appear to be great enthusiasm for the business, perhaps because of actuarial considerations. The Government-sponsored Finance For Industry, which draws its funds, for the most part, from City institutions, is another source of medium-term bank finance, but it is a demanding lender, with particularly stringent conditions which must be satisfied before any advance can be made.

Very substantial sums of medium-term bank finance are made available by banks, including accepting houses, insurance companies and other lending institutions. However, availability of such finance depends very largely on market conditions: when money is tight, there is a perceptible degree of reluctance to consider medium-term loans. In these circumstances, many U.K. companies have had to look for finance elsewhere than in the form of money borrowed within the U.K. Some of the instruments to which these companies turn when seeking medium-term finance, or security of supply of credit, are strictly sources of short-term credit: the obvious examples are bank overdrafts and acceptance credits. Not all medium-term finance is provided by banks or other financial institutions. It is possible to argue, albeit rather perversely, that most industrial companies are in receipt of a diminishing medium-term loan from the Government in the tax deferred as a result of the 100% allowance for tax in the first year after the capital spending takes place.

Leasing

Leasing is a particularly attractive form of medium-term finance for those companies who are themselves unable to claim the benefit of the 100% first-year capital allowances. The vast majority of banks in the U.K. are able to claim against their taxable profits the 100% first-year allowance available on equipment which they purchase. Competition in the leasing market is such that almost all the benefit of the tax deferral is passed on to the lessee company and reflected in a low rental. Rentals may be either fixed for the term, which may be as long as ten years, or geared to the lessor banks' funding costs. Leasing finance is of such importance that it is dealt with in much greater detail in a separate chapter, Chapter 15.

As in the first edition, the subject of loans to property and shipping companies (which may be in the form of medium-term finance) is dealt with under separate headings below.

Loans to Property Companies

Essentially, banks are not long-term lenders to property companies, although they do provide facilities of one kind or another over long periods. More frequently banks provide medium-term loans to property companies, which, in general, fall into one of two main categories. The first is development finance for specific or general developments, with substantial projects usually being financed in phases, so that the commencement of each new phase is dependent upon the successful completion of the previous phase. The second category includes lending for general investment purposes, *i.e.* to enable companies to retain and add to their portfolio developed and let properties.

There are many ways in which a loan may be structured. Partly as a matter of tradition and partly due to the medium-term nature of a development, loans to property companies are invariably on a secured basis whereby the bank advances a proportion of the required finance with the customer providing the balance from his own resources, thus creating the margin of security that is required by a lender. In general, loans are limited to approximately two-thirds of the finance required, although it is not unknown for banks to provide 100% of the finance, relying upon other property assets to provide the necessary margin.

The conditions attaching to medium-term property development loans will allow for interest to be capitalised during the development period and the lender will look for repayment within, say, a year of completion of the development, either from a sale to a third party or as a result of a funding operation with an insurance company or a pension fund.

Overall, property developers have tended to be an optimistic breed, but the experience of recent years has shown beyond any doubt that survival in the long term depends upon the ability to generate sufficient liquidity to meet a temporary cash shortfall. Furthermore, developments require tenants and the ease with which they are found tends to reflect the overall economic climate. Nevertheless, volatility in market sentiment can in the short term be accentuated and it is essential that the viability study for any such loan should allow for sufficient time in which to find a tenant and effect a funding.

Finally, loans for general investment purposes are more in the nature of working than development capital and the lender, while requiring a similar margin of security as in a development situation, will, in addition, stipulate that such security is fully developed and substantially let and that there is sufficient free rental income available to pay interest charges up to a given level.

Shipping Finance

Much of the medium-term finance provided by banks in recent years has gone into the shipping industry. Shipowners, who operate in a capital-intensive business which has shown an above-average rate of growth through the post-war period, have a continual need to finance the acquisition of vessels; in this their requirements are not dissimilar to those of property investment companies.

Like property companies, and unlike most manufacturers, they invest for the most part in assets for which a developed market exists, and which can therefore be considered more readily realisable than the book debts, stock, machinery and specialised buildings which constitute the major assets of most manufacturing companies. By charging those assets as security, they are able to obtain a higher level of debt in relation to their equity base than a manufacturing company could, particularly if the vessels (or properties) in question have a predetermined income.

Unlike property companies, however, shipping companies are more heavily reliant on bank finance. This is partly because ships, unlike land and buildings, depreciate quickly, and can be expected to be worth no more after 20 years or so than the scrap value of the metal of which they are built. Thus, they provide no more secure a hedge against inflation for the long-term investor than does any other piece of machinery.

At the same time the investor who is looking to the shipping industry for a satisfactory return on his capital over a shorter period is confronted with a highly volatile market in which asset values can halve and cash flows deteriorate from strong surplus to deep deficit within months. Since the average return on capital of the industry is not particularly high, the choice for most investors is between active participation in a shipping company and staying out of the sector altogether.

The most important factor restricting the access of shipowners to sources of long-term finance is the extreme fragmentation of the shipping industry. Only a small number of the largest shipping companies are strong enough to attract the non-specialist investor and many of them have been obliged to diversify in recent years to achieve a more acceptable return on capital and earnings trend. For the majority of family-controlled companies, their bankers represent the only external source of capital.

Most of the banks involved to any extent in the shipping sector have their own specialist ship finance departments. A high degree of expertise is necessary, as a shipping loan is normally a "project" loan; that is to say it is raised to finance a specific venture and is repaid from the profits of that venture. The bank's analysis of the project it is financing is therefore more critical than in the case of a loan (whether secured or unsecured) raised by a company as part of its general borrowing programme and repayable out of corporate cash flow.

Accordingly, in analysing a shipping loan a lender's primary concern is with future cash flow. When a vessel has been fixed on long-term charter this can be assessed with reasonable confidence, but account must be taken of the possibility that operating expenses or interest costs may rise faster than the hire paid by the charterer, with a consequent reduction in the surplus available to the owner for loan repayments. In such a proposal the financial strength of the charterer is naturally a vital consideration. Where no fixed long-term employment exists analysis must include the lender's own view, formed on the basis of his knowledge of the market, of the future earning capacity of the vessel and of its prospective value, as well as his assessment of the worth and ability of the shipowner.

Export Finance

So far, we have been concerned with the forms of medium-term finance that are available to U.K. companies but it should not be forgotten that the services of an accepting house are as open to foreign companies as to domestic ones. For the foreign buyer of U.K. capital goods and/or services, medium-term and often fixed interest rate finance can be arranged with the support of the Export Credits Guarantee Department (E.C.G.D.), which administers the scheme to encourage the purchase of British goods by foreign buyers and which is responsible to the Secretary of State for Trade.

Many industrialised countries, in order to encourage the growth of their export business, which is of vital importance because of the foreign exchange that it earns, have set up schemes to assist the exporter in a variety of ways. There are essentially three elements in the British scheme administered by the E.C.G.D. The first element is the simple insurance aspect, which assists the free flow of international trade by assuring the exporter of payment for goods shipped or services rendered if the buyer defaults for commercial reasons or as a result of a political upheaval. The second is the provision of that insurance, either to the exporter or to him and his bankers, in a form that facilitates the raising of finance for the transaction. The third element historically has been the interest subsidy on much export business financed under medium-term credit facilities. In return for issuing insurance cover, the E.C.G.D. charges the exporter a premium.

Two main criteria determine the nature of the services available to exporters from the E.C.G.D. First, business on which insurance is arranged on a purely commercial basis falls under Section I of the *Export Guarantees and Overseas Investment Act*, 1978, and other business which is considered desirable as a public service and in the national interest falls under Section II of the same Act. Secondly, the credit terms offered to exporters and their customers differ according to whether the business is short term and possibly repetitive, or whether it must, because of the nature and size of the order, be financed on extended terms of more than two years' credit.

Virtually all business done on terms of two years or less is covered on a comprehensive basis, where separate documentation in the form of specific financial agreements need not be drawn up for each order. British banks have agreed with the Government to finance 100% of the principal value of such business against the security of an E.C.G.D. comprehensive bill guarantee and at a preferential rate of interest, currently a maximum of ⅝% over each bank's base rate. This, the straightforward side of export finance, accounts for about 80% of all the E.C.G.D.'s business (the E.C.G.D., in turn, insures about one-third of all British exports).

The clearing banks dominate the short-term finance scene, with the confirming houses also playing a useful role, but the accepting houses have been very active in arranging medium-term finance for the benefit of their clients based on the E.C.G.D. guarantees – a large proportion of the finance made available through the

E.C.G.D. in the form of buyer credit continues to be arranged by them.

Medium- and long-term export finance is provided essentially in three different kinds of "package": in straightforward buyer or supplier credit for the purchase of individual capital goods items; in the form of a line of credit, where a single overseas buyer or a number of clients of a single financial institution can purchase a variety of capital goods from a number of British exporters through the use of the line; or in the form of project finance, where long-term export finance would be only one of the sources of finance tapped by a project that aimed to be viable from the start without recourse to the financial strength of third-party guarantors.

Before proceeding to a discussion of different applications of export finance, for instance, in lines of credit and project finance, it is important to understand two important common features of both buyer and supplier credits and also the essential differences between them. From the point of view of the overseas buyer, probably the most important feature of both supplier and buyer credit, is that, first, they may be made available in either sterling, U.S. dollars or Deutschmarks, at the borrower's option (and in exceptional circumstances, other hard currencies) and, secondly, except for credits to buyers in the European Economic Community, they bear interest at a fixed rate, which is normally subsidised. The fixed rate for each contract is selected by the E.C.G.D. in accordance with internationally agreed guidelines, at present within the range of 10 to 12.4% per annum, according to whether the borrower's country falls within the category of "poor", "intermediate" or "rich" based on a per capita income. Since April 1980, the finance required may be provided by recognised banks under the *Banking Act*, 1979 and in certain cases, with the consent of the E.C.G.D., by licensed deposit-takers.

The E.C.G.D. undertakes to continue funding foreign currency loans if a lending bank is precluded from raising sufficient funds on the Euromarkets. The banks receive a subsidy "interest make-up" equal to the difference between the fixed interest payable by the overseas borrower and interest at the rate at which the banks are able to obtain funds in the London Interbank Market (LIBOR) plus a margin (profit element) fixed by the E.C.G.D. For loans in sterling, the subsidy is based on an average of three months LIBOR plus a margin of 7/8% per annum, though this margin increases for loans with a repayment period in excess of twelve years, the margin being 1% per annum for that part of the loan repaid after the twelfth year. For loans in U.S. dollars or Deutschmarks the subsidy is based on six months LIBOR plus a margin ranging from ⅜ to ⅞% per annum, depending on the period of the loan. For other currencies special interest make-up arrangements may exist. The E.C.G.D. pays the subsidy to the banks at regular intervals with funds received from the Treasury. If the amount of fixed-rate interest payable by the overseas borrower exceeds the interest due to the banks at the relevant LIBOR rate plus the margin, then the banks must pay the excess to the E.C.G.D. This is, in fact, interest make-up in reverse. The interest margins are kept under review by the E.C.G.D. to see that they do not fall out of line with those prevailing in similar markets.

The nature of the transaction between the exporting company and its customer will differ according to whether the buyer or supplier credit form is to be used. The essence of supplier credit is that the exporter supplies goods to an overseas customer on a credit basis, receiving from the buyer a cash sum normally amounting to 15% or 20% of the value of the contract. The balance of the contract price is paid in six-monthly instalments over the relevant credit period and these instalments are secured by bills of exchange or promissory notes, the payment of which the supplier insures through the E.C.G.D. to 90% of their value, inclusive of interest. The supplier then sells the instruments on a without-recourse basis to his bank or to an accepting house which may have arranged a syndicate to purchase such instruments. The bank obtains a separate 100% guarantee direct from the E.C.G.D., the specific bank guarantee (S.B.G.). If the buyer fails to pay, the E.C.G.D. pays the bank under the S.B.G. and is entitled to recover from the exporter the relevant amount, leaving the exporter with the responsibility of claiming back from the E.C.G.D. up to 90% or 95% of the loss (depending on the cause of loss) under his E.C.G.D. insurance policy. The exporter, therefore, stands to lose only to a limited extent if the buyer does, in fact, default, providing his insurance claim is valid. Supplier credit accounts for a very high proportion of finance for capital goods contracts of between £50,000 and £2 million sold on extended terms credit, for which the credit period is generally restricted to five years from shipment of the goods or, sometimes, commissioning of the plant, where the supplier has contractual responsibility for such commissioning services. For larger contracts a buyer credit is normally preferred for reasons of contingent liability and the possibility of the supplier being able to claim progress payments during the course of manufacture.

The essence of buyer credit is that the exporter negotiates his contract with his buyer on a cash basis. The buyer finds from his own resources some 15 to 20% of the contract price (for which purpose he may raise separate "front-end" finance at a commercial and floating interest rate) and either he or his banker negotiates a separate loan agreement with an approved bank to provide the funds needed to make payment to the exporter of the balance of 80 to 85%. The approved bank secures from the E.C.G.D. an unconditional guarantee in respect of both principal and interest due from the buyer or the financial institution acting as borrower on his behalf. Buyer credit facilities are available for contracts of £1 million (or currency equivalent) and above, but are most generally used for much larger contracts for which extended repayment periods – in the case of very large contracts perhaps as long as 15 years from the commissioning of the plant – are negotiable, except that credits to industrialised countries normally attract a repayment period which is restricted to five years, even for larger contracts.

The buyer may also be able to secure additional fixed interest rate finance on the same terms under the loan agreement with the approved bank to assist in the finance of the local costs which are directly associated with the goods to be exported from the United Kingdom. The amount of such finance is usually limited to around 10 to 15% of the value of U.K. exports.

Suppliers find a number of advantages in buyer credits: for instance, progress payments are easier to arrange, and the problems of recourse by the E.C.G.D. on the supplier are much less onerous than under the supplier credit system. Buyer credits are also better suited to some buyers' business methods. However, there is no doubt that the documentation involved in buyer credits is more complicated than that for supplier credits. There is a lengthy loan agreement, which is subject to detailed checking by the E.C.G.D., which also checks the supply contract to ensure both that it fulfils a number of the E.C.G.D.'s basic requirements and also that it is compatible with the provisions of the loan agreement. The latter point is particularly important because disbursements from the loan are made direct to the exporter by the bank upon presentation of claims for work done or goods shipped under the contract in accordance with a procedure agreed in the contract, and this system effectively provides the exporter with a guarantee of payment as well as the buyer with medium-term finance.

It is therefore in this more complicated field of buyer credit that the skill of the accepting houses particularly comes into play (some accepting houses are active in supplier credits, but this is an area which is generally dominated by the clearing banks). In this field, an accepting house can offer an especially efficient and comprehensive service. Since it is mandatory to approach the E.C.G.D. before concluding any contract, a large number of variables – all interdependent – are all discussed at once. An intimate knowledge of the E.C.G.D.'s criteria is important to enable optimum use to be made of the services that it offers: this objective can be achieved by skilled drafting of the commercial contract and of the loan agreement between the buyer (or the institution borrowing funds on his behalf) and the bank or the leader of the syndicate of banks providing the funds. By working closely with the exporter on the various aspects of a buyer credit operation an accepting house can make an immediate contribution to the exporter's sales effort, particularly by ensuring that the buyer understands and makes use of the advantages offered by the U.K. export finance system. In addition, an accepting house can offer other services to the buyer; for instance, especially where the contract is exceptionally large, it may be able to arrange a total package including other export credits, currency facilities and local currency loans, as well as "front-end" finance to help the buyer meet the direct cash payment that he must make. Additionally, it can advise on the best currency in which to bid and ways of covering currency risks and of taking the best advantage of the forward exchange markets. Eurodollar borrowings, which are covered elsewhere (*see* Chapter 11), are the commonest source of front-end funds provided for this purpose through the medium of the bank arranging the finance. None of these services is unique, but an accepting house that is active in the field of export finance offers, as a result of its experience and its inherently flexible nature, an efficient service that is tailored to the demands of each individual contract. Furthermore, a number of accepting houses, as has already been said, have particular knowledge of certain areas of the world based on a traditional involvement in these areas which has given them a widespread experience of dealing with the countries concerned over a period of many years.

As already mentioned, the funds for both supplier and buyer credits may now be provided by recognised banks and sometimes licensed deposit-takers. In the case of syndicated loans an agent bank, normally a recognised bank and also a lender, negotiates and manages the loan throughout its life on behalf of all the lenders and for its services charges a negotiation fee payable on loan signature and an annual management fee. Sometimes the two fees are combined into a flat fee payable once only on loan signature. Sometimes, also, the role of arranging bank and agent bank are separate. There is also a commitment commission payable to the lending banks, calculated on the unutilised amount of the loan. The negotiation, management and commitment fees are usually paid by the exporter in the case of supplier credits and by the buyer in the case of buyer credits.

Buyer credits and supplier credits as described above envisage finance being organised for a single contract concluded at the same time as the loan agreement. However, there may be occasions when the buyer wishes to place a number of contracts which might or might not all be related to a single project, and it may not be practicable for all these to be concluded at the outset. In such a case it may be possible for him to arrange a line of credit to cover multiple contracts. A line of credit is operated on a buyer credit basis and covers contracts which can have a minimum value as low as £25,000 placed over, say, a 12- to 24-month period. By bulking together orders, the cover for which would otherwise have been considered separately by the E.C.G.D., somewhat better credit terms may be available than would be obtained for individual contracts. The arrangement also offers a considerable convenience to the buyer since the negotiation of individual credit terms on each contract is already secured. The E.C.G.D. would normally expect to be satisfied that the issuing of a line of credit will bring additional business to U.K. exporters. Once the line of credit is set up, individual contracts are subsequently approved by the borrower and lender as eligible to be financed from the credit. The supplier can then be paid up to a fixed percentage of the U.K. content of his contract from the loan.

The terms of repayment of a line of credit will vary from between two and five years, according to the nature and size of the contracts financed and, in the case of project lines of credit, can be as favourable as the repayment terms for a large single contract.

The role of the accepting house is much the same as in a normal buyer credit except that a bank will on many occasions have as its client the overseas buyer rather than any particular U.K. exporter: in arranging lines of credit, accepting houses are often paving the way for exporters by eliminating in advance possible financing difficulties.

Project Finance

In arranging buyer credit finance and lines of credit, the E.C.G.D. and the British banks who operate the scheme concern themselves with individual U.K. capital contracts or with a variety of such contracts. To an increasing extent, however, buyers are seeking finance for major "green-field" projects. Project finance is a much-abused term and, in some cases, appears to mean little more than straightforward buyer credit, but among banks who are more seriously committed to project finance it involves the arrange-ment, from a variety of sources, of the finance necessary to appraise, supply and construct a large capital project. In some cases, where accurate forecasts can be made of the future financial results of the project company, it may be possible to arrange the finance on a non-recourse basis – that is to say in such a way that the financial security for the loans made to the project company derives from future assured cash flows, and is independent of the financial strength of the promoting organisation, whether it be a commercial company or a government agency.

The beginning of this chapter discussed very briefly the major sources of medium-term finance before looking in rather more detail at export credit and the part that the accepting houses can play in arranging the provision of such finance. In project finance, this broad view is all-important, since the variety of potential sources of finance is very great. In many cases a government agency will wish to hold some but not all of the equity, and will hope to attract an experienced overseas partner to supply some of the equity capital and to manage the plant and possibly market the product, thus ensuring the enthusiasm of the operating partner. The promoters of the project will therefore need advice about the amount of equity capital required – a complex question, the answer to which will depend on the size of the project and its nature, and how economically various forms of debt can be arranged – and how it should be split between the operating partners. Simultaneously, it is necessary to seek out all the sources of debt finance and aid, beginning, perhaps, with the World Bank and the European Investment Bank, which may provide finance for government projects, or with the International Finance Corporation, the arm of the World Bank dealing with non-government projects, and with the various regional development banks in certain parts of the world. Other institutions which may be approached at various times include government agencies, national export finance organisations (the U.S. Eximbank and the French Coface, to name but two that perform a similar function to the British E.C.G.D.), local capital markets, the Eurocurrency market, and bank syndicates for the provision of leasing services and term loans. In attempting to arrange finance on the security of the future cash flows from the project, it will almost certainly be essential to show advance sales contracts for part of the planned production: it will be necessary actively to seek these, and to arrange them in a way that is acceptable to both buyer and seller, using suitable option and default clauses.

There are, therefore, many interlocking considerations that need to be borne in mind when attempting to arrange the finance for large capital projects. Although the accepting houses were not the first in this field (U.S. banks arranging finance for oilfields probably have that honour), they have made a name for themselves as expert financial advisers to projects. Although the concept of a project which itself generates the security for the loans made to the company or agency that owns it is a neat and intellectually satisfying one, the actual process of arranging such a package calls for a detailed understanding of the project and the potential problems involved, patience and tenacity on the part of all those who are involved and, in addition, for real diplomatic skill on the part of the advisers!

Project finance is not a well-defined method of fund-raising, but rather an evaluation, using a systematic approach, of the possibilities and options applicable to any one project. Computer models for sensitivity analysis and for the forecasting of cash flows and all financial aspects of a project have become widely available. As the pace of development quickens in the underdeveloped countries, and as the capital cost of projects continues to rise (due partly to inflation, but more importantly to an increase in the size of projects considered economically viable), the difficult art of project finance will continue to gain in importance. It seems likely that the accepting houses will remain the major British force in what is already an international and highly competitive business.

8

LONG-TERM AND PERMANENT FINANCE, MERGERS AND ACQUISITIONS

✐

New issues on the one hand and mergers and acquisitions on the other, although they may seem to be quite distinct, have many features in common. While it is convenient to consider them separately, both are subject to the same financial, legal and other disciplines and are normally handled by the same department within an accepting house. This department, often called the house's "corporate" or "company finance division", exists to provide its corporate clients with advice and assistance on many of the financial, and sometimes the non-financial, aspects of their activities. It tends to be staffed by people with professional backgrounds, for example, chartered accountants and lawyers, as well as by those with industrial and commercial backgrounds. New issues, mergers and acquisitions are only a part, albeit often a much publicised part, of the division's business. It is able to offer not only technical expertise, but also the wealth of its own experience over a broad range of problems and so to provide its clients with a perspective they would not find elsewhere.

New Issues

In outline, the new issue business of the accepting houses involves the sponsoring of capital issues and the sale of securities to the public, either in the United Kingdom or overseas.

Generally speaking, companies have three sources of funds: banks; institutional investors, such as insurance companies, pension funds and investment trusts; and individual investors.

This chapter is concerned with the last two categories who are interested primarily in marketable securities. It is the accepting house's business, as an issuing house, to bring investors and companies together. These may be companies coming to the market for the first time or companies wishing to issue further shares or marketable debt.

The accepting house has several important roles to perform in this exercise. As financial adviser to a company it is likely to be involved in helping to plan its client's financing strategy. With its knowledge of the market it will be closely concerned with advising on the terms, amount and timing of any issue, as well as the type of security appropriate to the company's requirements and market conditions. Its knowledge of the technicalities, legal and other, means that it will have much to do with the detailed preparation of the documentation. Its public association with an issue can be crucial, since investors may pay considerable regard to the reputation of the sponsoring bank in considering the issue's merits. And finally, as described below, the bank will put itself financially at risk by underwriting an issue.

The First Public Issue

Companies coming to the market for the first time are most likely to be involved in the issue of ordinary shares. Subsequently they may be involved in the issue of other securities, including not only share capital (which itself can comprise preference as well as ordinary shares), but also marketable debt, for example, debentures, unsecured loan stocks or loan stocks convertible into ordinary shares.

There is no single reason why a company should want to sell its shares to the public and seek a stock market listing. In most cases the arguments for doing so include the need to raise fresh capital, the desire of the existing owners to realise a part of their shareholdings and the wish to secure the greater marketability which a company's shares will have once they are listed (which in turn bears upon the company's ability, not only to make further issues for cash or acquisitions, but also, in the longer term, to survive its original owners and maintain independence and continuity of business).

Any company coming to the market for the first time must satisfy certain criteria, the chief of which are satisfactory management, a proven record over a number of years, sound future prospects, an appropriate corporate and capital structure, an expected market value of at least £500,000 and an indicated dividend policy. The governing regulations are set out in The Stock Exchange's "Yellow Book" *Admission of Securities to Listing* and in the Companies Acts.

There are several other factors which can materially affect the successful issue of a company's shares. These include the sponsorship of a reputable issuing house and/or stockbroker, the appointment of good firms of solicitors and reporting chartered accountants and the general reputation of the company and its products. The association of an accepting house or other issuing house with such a company is likely to have preceded the issue itself by a matter of at least months and often years. The accepting house will not only have been involved in helping the company prepare specifically for a listing: the decision to seek a listing may itself have emerged as part of a broader strategy formed in consultation with the accepting house.

The preparation for a listing is time-consuming, if only because of the utmost importance of ensuring that the prospectus is both completely accurate and discloses everything that prospective investors should know. The investigations made prior to an issue by the sponsoring bank and the accountants and solicitors it employs have to be very thorough.

Methods of Issue

There are three normal methods by which a company can obtain a listing on The Stock Exchange: the most common is an offer for sale, the others being an introduction and (most rarely) a placing. The Stock Exchange normally requires at least 25% of the company's share capital to be in the hands of the public.

Under an offer for sale an issuing house will buy shares in the company at a certain price and will then offer the shares to the public at a marginally higher price, the difference representing the issuing house's commission and its own expenses. The issuing house's commission is in turn heavily reduced by the commission paid to the stockbrokers and sub-underwriters, whose role is described below. The shares thus purchased and offered may be either new shares or shares already in issue and held by the original shareholders: in the former case it is the company which will receive the cash proceeds of sale; in the latter case it is the original shareholders.

An introduction is less common and does not involve the sale of shares to the public. Broadly speaking it can be the most appropriate method when the securities are already listed on another stock exchange, or where an unlisted company has reached such a size in terms of capitalisation and spread of shareholders as to fulfil The Stock Exchange's marketability criteria or where, as a variant of the latter, an introduction follows a private placing of the company's shares.

The placing method is commonly used to sell loan stock rather than shares, the reason being that it is normally only allowed by The Stock Exchange when there is not likely to be significant demand from the general public for the securities being marketed. It is none the less convenient to describe it at this point. There is no general offer to the public. The issuing house will, for a commission, enter into a commitment to find purchasers of the loan stock and, if they cannot be found, to buy the stock itself. The normal buyers of marketable debt are institutional investors with whom the issuing house places the stock, at the same time arranging to have it listed. In most instances The Stock Exchange requires that some of the securities being placed are made available to the market, so that any members of the public who wish to subscribe may do so through their brokers.

The Unlisted Securities Market (the U.S.M.) was launched by The Stock Exchange in 1980 to provide a public market for the shares in smaller companies who are not able, or do not wish, to apply for the full listing. The requirements are significantly less onerous than for a full listing. For example, only 10% of the shares are required to be in the hands of the public and a company must normally have a trading record (and audited accounts) for at least a three-year period, compared with the normal requirement of at least five years for a full listing. In addition, if no shares are being offered to the public at the time of a company's entry on to the U.S.M., no accountant's report on the company's record is required. However, if shares are to be "marketed", then the prospectus requirements are no different from those applying to a full listing.

Pricing and Underwriting

The pricing of a new issue is of crucial importance. The existing owners have an obvious interest in obtaining the highest price possible. On the other hand, too high a price may make the issue unattractive to investors and damage the company's reputation, among other things impairing its ability to raise money from the market on a future occasion. It is for the issuing house to advise on price against the market background on the one hand, and the characteristics of the company on the other (the nature of its business, reputation, profits, dividend policy and so on). This is not an easy task.

The company (or the selling shareholders) under an offer for sale or placing will have been assured by the issuing house of receiving the proceeds of sale and so be protected against the possibility of the issue being unsuccessful. This is achieved by the issuing house (before the offer is made public) assuming a liability as underwriter of the issue to buy any securities remaining unsold at the end of the offer or placing period. As already described, the mechanics of an offer for sale and of a placing can be different: in an offer for sale the issuing house buys the securities which are to be offered to the public and retains any which are unsold, while, under the placing method, the offer to the placees may technically be made on behalf of the company, the issuing house agreeing to buy any securities left unsold. In either event the liability of the issuing house is effectively the same.

While the issuing house carries this underwriting liability for the period of the offer or placing, in the case of the former it will usually arrange for the issue to be sub-underwritten by investing institutions (such as insurance companies and pension funds) who receive a commission from the issuing house for agreeing to buy shares not taken up by the public. These are very often the same institutions to whom securities are sold under the placing method.

The issuing house's ability, however, to find sub-underwriters and placees depends on its pricing record. An issue which is unsuccessful in the sense that it is in part left with sub-underwriters and opens in the market at a discount to the subscription price may affect the issuing house's reputation adversely. On the other hand, an issue which opens at an excessive premium may disappoint the issuing company or selling shareholders for whom the issuing house is acting, since the premium indicates a greater demand for the securities than was allowed for in the pricing of the issue.

The problem of pricing can be particularly acute in a volatile market. An attempt to solve the problem when prices generally in the stock market are rising sharply, or when the nature of the issuing company's business is such that no comparison can be properly made with any other listed companies, has been the offer for sale by tender under which those wishing to subscribe apply for the shares at a price of their own choosing at or above a fixed minimum price.

Variants of Company Capital Structure

Once a company is quoted on The Stock Exchange it can increase its equity capital either as a result of acquiring assets, including the share capital of other companies, in exchange for the issue of shares (as discussed in the following section on mergers and acquisitions), or by a further issue of shares for cash. As described later, the company also has the opportunity through the issue of marketable debt to create a new and longer form of debt structure not always open to an unlisted company, whose sources of lending are generally confined to shorter-term bank finance.

Further issues of ordinary shares for cash are generally confined by the Companies Acts and The Stock Exchange to offers by way of rights to existing shareholders in proportion to their shareholdings, unless the shareholders approve otherwise. The subscription price is usually fixed at a discount to the market price, but cannot by law be less than par value. Although the shares issued are not normally acquired by the issuing house involved, but offered directly to the shareholders, the company can be assured from the start that the shares will be taken up because the issue will usually have been underwritten by the issuing house and in turn sub-underwritten by a wide range of investing institutions.

The marketable debt of companies in the United Kingdom can be divided into three main types of loan stock: unsecured; secured by a floating charge on the assets; and secured by a fixed charge on certain assets (normally property). The stock usually has a term of 15 years and more (with or without sinking fund) and the interest rate is fixed to final maturity. The stock is set up under a trust deed establishing the rights of the holders and certain restrictions to which the company has agreed to conform; a trustee (often an insurance company) is appointed to look after the holders' interests.

Convertible loan stocks and loan stocks with warrants attached provide companies and investors with alternatives to both straight debt and equity. The former carry a right over a period of years under which the holder can choose to convert the stock into ordinary shares at a predetermined conversion price. At the time of issue the conversion price is fixed almost invariably at a premium over the then current share price while the interest rate is fixed at a level above the current dividend yield on the shares. Nevertheless, because of the added appeal to the investor of the right of conversion, the interest rate is likely to be lower than it would need to be for a comparable straight debt issue.

A loan stock with warrants is similar in essence to the convertible and like a convertible it carries a lower coupon than a straight loan stock. The difference is that its conversion right (the warrant) may be detached and quoted separately; the warrant can be converted or exercised at a predetermined exercise price payable either in cash or, in some cases, by the surrender of the appropriate nominal amount of loan stock or a combination of both. The attraction of a warrant is that its value is geared to the price of the underlying equity, but payment is deferred until the date of exercise which, at the holder's option, can stretch over a period of some years. An issue of a convertible loan stock or a loan stock with warrants is, for the reasons that apply to an issue of ordinary shares, generally confined to offers by way of rights to existing shareholders.

The convertible loan stock and loan stock with warrants attached have also been used by the United Kingdom subsidiaries of foreign companies to raise sterling funds in the London market. The common practice has been for the subsidiary (using the placing method) to issue sterling loan stock, convertible into the shares of its parent company.

Mergers and Acquisitions

One of the more publicised activities of the accepting houses and other issuing houses is their involvement as advisers in the field of take-overs and mergers. In practice a bank's involvement in a particular merger or acquisition, both as adviser to and agent of its client, is likely to have begun long before the public stage is reached. A specific proposal may have emerged as part of a broader corporate strategy established with the help of the issuing house, which is also likely to have been closely and directly involved in the negotiations leading up to an offer. Indeed, a large part of the negotiations may have been conducted not between the principals, but between two issuing houses on their behalf. One of the advantages of this arrangement is that it can help to produce a greater degree of flexibility and understanding between the parties, as well as a forum for unemotional argument.

Many proposals founder at this stage for lack of commercial

justification or for price or other reasons. The majority of acquisitions or mergers which come before shareholders for their acceptance have already been agreed between the directors of both companies. However, there are a significant number of cases where an acquisition is publicly proposed by one company, but opposed by the other. The advantages of agreement are, first, that it can be counter-productive to acquire a company whose management has publicly opposed the offer and, second, that a publicly contested offer is more likely to bring in third parties.

There are several reasons for making, accepting or opposing a take-over bid or a proposal to merge. A company may wish to acquire or merge with another to enhance or to protect its own market position, to expand vertically or horizontally, to diversify into new products or geographical areas, to acquire assets which it believes it can employ more profitably than the current owner, or for a combination of any of these and other reasons. Equally a company may be opposed to being acquired because it considers the price inadequate, because it values its commercial independence, because it takes a different view than the acquiring company of the latter's or its own prospects, because of apparent differences in management styles, or, again, for a combination of reasons. A bid situation may be complicated by the intervention of a counter-bidder or by the original bidder, seeing that his original bid may fail, desiring to raise his offer.

There are two principal methods of effecting an acquisition or a merger. The more common is for the acquiring company (the offeror) to make an offer for the whole of the share capital of the other (the offeree). The other is for shareholders to be asked to agree to a scheme of arrangement under the Companies Acts.

It is usual under the offer method for the offer to be made by an issuing house on behalf of the offeror; and where a merger is effected by the scheme method an issuing house will often have the responsibility of providing shareholders with the explanatory statement of what is proposed. In either event, in order that the shareholders should be in a position to decide on the merits of an offer or intention to merge, there has to be a full presentation of the facts and the reasons for what is proposed with reference to the advantages, such as rationalisation and savings, that can be expected to ensue. An issuing house will often play an important part in presenting such information to shareholders or, in an opposed bid, in presenting the counter-arguments.

The social considerations of acquisitions and mergers have

become increasingly important over the years. The question of monopoly, the effect upon consumer choice and the implications for employees are subject to considerable scrutiny. At the same time the technical aspects of acquisitions and mergers have become more complicated. The form of consideration paid by the acquiring company, be it shares, convertible stock, warrants, debt, cash or some combination of these, can have a significant impact both on the financial outcome of a proposal on the acquiring company and on its acceptability or otherwise to the shareholders in the company being acquired. It will be for the issuing house to help devise a package which satisfies both parties.

The bank is also in a position to guide its client through the many regulations affecting mergers and take-overs, including those relating to the acquisition of shares in the offeree company before and during the take-over. These are regulations imposed either by City bodies such as the Council for the Securities Industry, the Panel on Take-overs and Mergers and The Stock Exchange or by governmental bodies, such as the Office of Fair Trading (whose function is to consider whether a take-over or merger should be referred to the Monopolies and Mergers Commission). The Companies and Taxation Acts can be equally relevant. The scale of the regulatory requirements reflects a general concern that both the manner in which mergers and take-overs are implemented and their social and economic consequences should be viewed from the standpoint of the public interest as well as that of the shareholders involved.

The Panel was itself set up in the late 1960s, in great part, it should be said, as a result of work by the accepting houses because of the City's anxiety about the manner in which certain take-overs had been conducted, and its basic philosophy that self-regulation is better than parliamentary legislation which tends to lead to the attitude of mind that what is not illegal is legal. In 1978, the Council for the Securities Industry was set up to formalise the co-ordination of the activities of the various sectors of the securities industry, including the Panel and The Stock Exchange. The Panel has a full-time professional executive staff, which deals with day-to-day enquiries and problems. The full Panel is made up of leading representatives from the City and business who meet together to consider matters of particular interest and to deliberate any cases where a company may dispute a decision of the executive. The rules of the Panel are published in a "City Code", which is amended from time to time in the light of prevailing circumstances. In offer documents, a summary has to be printed of the rules of the Panel relating to the length of time that an offer may be open and setting out what rights of withdrawal are available to shareholders.

Summarising, a take-over or merger can be subject to considerable financial, technical and administrative complications, on all of which a company will require expert advice and assistance if it is to achieve whatever is in its best interests. Furthermore, it is an area of business which by its nature rarely proceeds smoothly. Accepting houses have an experience and expertise which it is not normally the client's business to possess and which enables them to make a unique contribution.

Recent years have seen the development of a class of acquisitions in which the management (and sometimes other employees) of a company buy its shareholding, either from the public or from a publicly owned company. In these transactions (often called management buy-backs) the vendors and the purchasers are commonly advised by merchant banks.

9

INTERNATIONAL ISSUES

The accepting houses have played a prominent part in the development of the international capital market since the Second World War. As advisers to borrowers their names are often to be found among the leading managers of an issue and such managers, as their description implies, carry the main responsibility for advising their clients on all the complexities of taxation, currency risk, interest rates, pricing, marketing, and legal documentation. The techniques employed in such issues are different from those employed in a U.K. issue and may involve either the syndication of the loan among a group of lending banks or the formation of a hierarchy of a managing group, an underwriting group and a selling group of banks, in any one or more of which the names of accepting houses are to be found.

International Capital Market

The Eurobond market, whose origins date back to 1963, is one of the major sources of medium- and long-term capital in the world. The annual volume of new issues has grown from a little over U.S. $1 billion in 1965 to more than U.S. $24 billion in 1981 and the total volume of financing raised now exceeds U.S. $160 billion or its equivalent in other currencies.

The Eurobond market is essentially a market for high-quality borrowers. It serves supranational organisations, governments and government entities which have traditionally financed a portion of their funding requirements outside their own domestic capital markets. High-quality commercial and industrial corporations have also made extensive use of the market as a means of diversifying their sources of funds or to take advantage of specific fund-raising opportunities which are not available to them in their own countries. The wide geographical spread of borrowers encompasses both the developed and less developed areas of the world.

The most widely used currency is the U.S. dollar. The U.S. dollar-denominated issues have typically accounted for between 60 and 80% of the overall volume of new issues in any one year. The second most important currency is the Deutschmark, but other currencies frequently used include the Canadian dollar, Dutch guilder, French franc, sterling, Swiss franc, yen, and a variety of composite currency units, such as the European Currency Unit and Special Drawing Rights and, to a lesser extent, a number of Middle Eastern currencies.

The majority of issues take the form of fixed interest rate securities. Issues which are convertible into the borrower's equity and floating rate note issues, whose interest is payable periodically by reference to short-term deposit interest rates, are also common. The increasing volatility of world currency exchange rates and interest rates in recent years has produced a number of new borrowing techniques, including issues providing the investor with the option of receiving interest payments in more than one currency, zero coupon and deep discount issues, and issues whose interest payment is linked to the price of oil or gold. The development of some of these techniques is still at an experimental stage. The size of individual issues varies considerably, but typically ranges from U.S. $50 to 100 million. Certain prime borrowers have on occasion been able to raise in excess of U.S. $500 million in one amount. Maturities are generally no shorter than five years and no longer than 15 years.

Eurobonds are negotiable obligations with detachable coupons for the payment of interest to bearer, free of withholding tax. The securities are usually denominated in amounts of U.S. $1,000 or U.S. $5,000 and interest is payable annually in the case of fixed-rate bonds and semi-annually in the case of floating-rate notes and convertible bonds. Public issues are usually listed either on the London or Luxembourg Stock Exchange.

Generally, however, issues are traded in an over-the-counter market maintained by a large number of banks and securities houses based in several European capitals, as well as in Hong

Kong, New York, Singapore and Tokyo. The U.K. financial community, particularly the accepting houses, has made an important contribution in encouraging the development of the Eurobond market since its inception and London remains the principal financial centre in which issues are arranged and traded.

Traditionally, a large proportion of the investment in Eurobonds has emanated from private individuals whose funds, large and small, are administered by commercial and investment banks. Since the mid-1970s the OPEC surpluses have been an important source of funds, as have the growing number of institutions around the world attracted to the market by the opportunities for currency diversification and the wide choice of issues which the Eurobond market offers.

U.K. Companies and the Capital Markets

Leading U.K. companies, in common with substantial foreign corporate entities, are able to borrow medium- and long-term funds in the Eurobond market and in the U.K. and other domestic capital markets. Typically, a U.K. company will borrow sterling to fund its domestic capital spending programme, but may also borrow in other currencies with a view to funding operations abroad, or in order to arrange a currency swap to obtain sterling or another desired currency. The accessibility of these capital markets, particularly the Eurobond market, is dependent on the borrowing company's capital being sufficiently large, at least in the order of £50 to 60 million. Furthermore, the company's existing debt issues must be rated such that the market will accept the company as a good credit risk. To ensure that the issue is a success, it is vital that the company's name is known to international investors.

For fiscal reasons, namely the payment of interest to investors free of withholding tax, the U.K. corporate borrower needs to establish a borrowing vehicle which would be incorporated offshore and would be wholly owned and guaranteed by the parent company. In general, the U.K. company will seek listing of the securities that it issues on the London Stock Exchange and it will, in order to comply with disclosure requirements, give details of the borrower, the guarantor and the terms and conditions of the securities that are being issued.

U.K. Domestic Sterling Market

The abolition in October 1979 of exchange controls, which had been in existence since the beginning of the Second World War, has opened the London market to non-U.K. borrowers (the "Bulldog" market) and has enabled U.K. institutions to invest freely abroad. Significantly, the Bulldog market provides borrowers with the opportunity to raise long-term sterling funds. To date, the majority of issues have carried maturities in excess of 20 years, although there have also been some issues with five-year maturities. The total amount raised by foreign entities since the market re-opened exceeds £1 billion. The amounts raised by individual issues have ranged between £15 million and £100 million.

The Bank of England regulates the flow of new Bulldog issues through the government broker. There are two principal methods of offering securities in the U.K. domestic market: namely a "placing" with institutions and an "offer for sale" to the public.

Eurosterling Market

The Eurosterling market re-opened in 1977 and, until the opening of the Bulldog market in 1979, provided the only source of fixed-rate sterling finance for overseas borrowers. The re-opening of the market came in response to an emerging interest by international investors in purchasing sterling as a currency and a simultaneous decline in interest rates in the U.K.

Eurosterling issues normally raise smaller equivalent amounts than Eurodollar issues in view of the generally more limited demand for sterling from both borrowers and investors. To date, some 55 issues have been launched in the Eurosterling market, two of them on a floating-rate basis, raising a total of about £1.3 billion with only four issues raising £50 million or more. The Eurosterling market in contrast to the domestic sterling market provides borrowers with funds in the medium-term range of five to fifteen years.

10

THE MERCHANT BANKS AND VENTURE CAPITAL

Definition of "Venture Capital"

The expression "venture capital" is normally used in a rather restricted sense in the U.K. and is taken to mean investment in new companies with no trading history. The financial community is inclined to regard this kind of investment as time-consuming and unprofitable, and in this respect it is sometimes contrasted unfavourably with "development capital" which is seen as entailing investment in mature and usually profitable businesses requiring finance either for expansion or diversification. In the United States, where venture capital has achieved considerable recent success, this distinction is rightly avoided: it is recognised that, in practice, the company requiring "venture capital" today (*i.e.* start-up finance) may require development capital tomorrow. It is therefore regarded as appropriate for both to be provided by similar sources.

Attitude of British Merchant Banks

Historically, merchant banks in the United Kingdom have tended to take a more sympathetic view of venture capital than the rest of the British financial community, although few merchant bankers could today be described as enthusiasts. Ironically, the popular image of merchant banks associates them closely with venture capital investment, an association which owes a good deal to a romantic idea that merchant bankers are really merchant venturers.

The principal business of merchant banks is, of course, banking rather than investment. Merchant banks are concerned to lend money on good security and at commercial rates of interest. Where they invest (*i.e.* acquire shares) in companies, it is generally as managers of other people's money (both private individuals and pension funds) and, when they do, they are usually investing in mature, publicly quoted companies rather than those which are new or at least young and inadequately financed. The mainstream of merchant banking may reasonably be described as "risk averse"; nevertheless, as a by-product of their banking, corporate advisory and investment management operations, merchant bankers are presented with an increasing flow of potentially attractive investment and speculative propositions, some of which can broadly be described as "venture capital".

Problems Entailed in Venture Capital

It often occurs that a young business approaches a merchant bank for loan finance where it finds that its principal bankers (usually a High Street branch of a clearing bank) are unwilling to lend. In this situation, the merchant bank will generally be unable to obtain the quality of security that it normally requires and the acquisition by it of an equity interest in the company may be seen as an appropriate compensation for the higher degree of risk involved in the loan. However, the conservative approach adopted by most bankers in assessing credit risks will seldom permit them to acquire an equity investment on this basis.

From the banking point of view, one of the main difficulties involved in lending to small companies is that the loans involved can be expensive and difficult to administer. From the point of view of the small company itself, it is often impractical to finance itself entirely with loans at, in recent years, punitive rates of interest: at the time when it most needs to conserve its resources, the payment of interest and even the repayment of the loan may begin.

It is significant that few members of the Accepting Houses Committee have joined the Government's Loan Guarantee Scheme, which provides a state guarantee to lending bankers on qualifying loans to small companies of up to £75,000. The reason for this is clear: most merchant banks find it uneconomic to administer loans of £150,000, let alone £75,000, and their enthusiasm for this type of lending, unaccompanied by any other business, is understandably muted. The provision of loan finance is therefore unattractive unless the bank is also involved as an investor (whether on its own account or on behalf of clients) or as corporate adviser.

Increased Interest in Venture Capital

In the last few years various factors have contributed to stimulate interest in venture capital and to encourage merchant bankers, among others, to become more interested in accommodating themselves to requirements for venture finance and associated banking and corporate advisory services. These considerations may well lead to a change in approach on the part of the merchant banks and they are worth examining in some detail.

In the U.S.A., venture capital investment made a great deal of progress before major brokerage firms and investment banks became involved. The widely perceived success of a number of small venture funds, financed largely by private individuals, has now sparked off an entire industry and broking firms and investment banks have recently been taking an increasingly active role both in setting up venture funds and assisting individual companies to raise finance.

The importance of private capital has been recognised by the British Government through the introduction of the Business Start-up Scheme, which enables private investors to reduce their taxable income to the extent of certain qualifying "venture capital" investments. Merchant bankers, as managers of private capital, now have a modest incentive to consider such investments on behalf of their private clients, although the extent of their interest has so far been limited. It might have been rather greater had there been adequate specialised investment funds available as a means of channelling the investment. Investing by means of a fund is widely regarded as appropriate because of its great advantage of spreading risk between a portfolio of investments, with a reasonable likelihood that a proportion of them will be successful and more than compensate for the failure or modest performance of the remainder. To date, the merchant banks have not taken a particularly active role in spawning U.K. venture capital funds, preferring, instead, to make isolated investments directly.

As many merchant banks tend to manage more corporate than private funds, and as the former cannot benefit from the Business Start-up Scheme, there is less incentive to look at venture capital propositions on behalf of corporate investment clients. Other pressures have nevertheless combined to stimulate their investment interest in venture capital; greater exposure to overseas markets, particularly to the U.S.A., has demonstrated that active venture capital investment can be an important element in the public market in securities through assisting the development of smaller high technology companies. Many merchant bank investment managers would like to follow the lead of some U.S. money managers in making investments in these companies at an earlier stage, often at the same time as venture capitalists are investing in them. Hence, since 1979 or thereabout, a number of merchant banks have invested some client funds in established U.S. venture capital organisations, and a more limited group have been active participants in U.S. venture capital, both by setting up their own funds and by direct participation in specific U.S. venture financings.

Recently, a common interest in venture capital has been developing between investment management and corporate finance departments. Both elements, reflecting on the U.S. experience, can see that the most important role that venture capital is likely to play lies in the development of the "industries of tomorrow". There are now a few signs that this process is getting under way in the U.K.; as it does, it will create a need for the additional financing of companies that prove that they are essentially viable, but require further working capital. At this stage they become potential clients of the corporate advisory departments of the merchant banks.

If domestic corporate finance activity in the U.K. were still at the level of the early 1970s, it is likely that the interest of corporate finance departments in such a source of new business would be fairly modest. However, the corporate advisory business of most merchant banks has suffered since 1973 from the relative decline of the new issue market. The recent increase in new issue activity has, in many cases, involved young companies, not all of whom have availed themselves of the services of a merchant bank in entering the public market (often by means of the Unlisted Securities Market). Most merchant banks see it as important not to ignore this market and are interesting themselves in the affairs of some relatively young and small businesses which they see as the seedcorn of their future.

Current Developments

The developments mentioned above are, of course, some way removed from direct investment by a merchant bank of its own funds, or even from the involvement of banking departments in loans to the companies concerned. An increased degree of interest will not translate itself into much practical involvement in an investment and banking sense until some new factor emerges as a catalyst: the essence of the U.S. venture capital business is the investment funds that have been springing into existence since 1973. The existence of the funds and their professional management teams has created a venture capital "community" of banks, brokers, corporate funds and technical experts. Without the existence of a similar "community", venture capital is unlikely to make rapid progress in the United Kingdom. The key question, then, is how its emergence can be accelerated and what role the merchant banks will play in its development. There is scope for merchant banks to act as sponsors of venture capital funds, to set up the management companies and to have equity interests in them. The U.S.-style funds (where the management will generally have a 20% "carried" or free interest in profits made by the fund) can be highly profitable for managers/sponsors.

Whether or not the merchant banks themselves set up the funds is not important as long as they are established: thereafter, the merchant banks will fulfil their natural role – as providers of finance for the funds themselves, as corporate advisers to the young companies, as a conduit for the raising of further finance by means of placing shares with major investing institutions, and, finally, as bankers.

PART THREE

MONEY MANAGEMENT

11

FOREIGN EXCHANGE

Development of the Foreign Exchange Market

The earliest method of conducting international trade was by means of barter, a straight exchange of one set of imported or exported goods for another. Gradually the development towards forms of foreign exchange took place. Travelling merchants accepted the currency of the country in which they were selling their goods, and used it to purchase local products. Eventually, this was followed by an exchange of one country's money in coin form for another's. As this was effected by weighing the coins, the rate at which the coins were exchanged was determined by their metal content; in fact, the transactions were bullion deals rather than exchange deals. From this developed the acceptance of one country's currency for another at a certain rate and thus the birth of the foreign exchange market.

As one examines the modern exchange market, it is as well to remember that the concepts of exchange control and fixed or floating exchange control and fixed or floating exchange rates are not new, but have been practised in one form or another, at one time or another, for at least 2,000 years. What is a relatively new concept is the utmost importance of an international monetary system functioning smoothly, able to handle and finance a large volume of international trade and investments. Consequently, the foreign exchange rate policy of most governments has become an important economic instrument, although its use has not always had the desired effect.

The London foreign exchange market was slow to develop. For

much of the last century markets in other European cities such as Amsterdam, Berlin and Vienna were far more important. As such a large proportion of the world's trade was invoiced and financed in sterling, the need to exchange sterling into the local currency arose in markets other than London. At the same time, sterling was a steady currency convertible into gold, whereas some of the European currencies were unstable.

Accepting houses and branches of foreign banks established in London were the backbone of the foreign exchange market and used to meet in the Royal Exchange. This practice was abandoned after the First World War, but in many European centres the practice of meeting daily in a stock exchange to establish official quotations for currencies is still being observed. Between the two world wars, London established a predominant position in the world's foreign exchange markets: its geographical position, large share of international trade, the use of sterling as a reserve currency and financing medium, its wide range of financial and allied services and its long-established and sound financial institutions are all factors which can be named as reasons for this development. The expertise in foreign exchange dealing that the accepting houses and branches of foreign banks had gained before the First World War was of great importance in achieving this dominant position. The close relations which most accepting houses had established with certain countries and their financial institutions were of great value. Indeed, some of these traditional links are still in evidence today and accepting houses, like other banks, tend to specialise in dealings in particular currencies.

Following the First World War, apart from the ill-fated return to the gold standard between 1925 and 1931, sterling was no longer convertible into gold and became less stable, so that more imports into the United Kingdom were invoiced in the currency of the seller: an expansion of the foreign exchange market from its pre-1914 era was therefore a natural consequence. It was then that the clearing banks, in order to service their commercial customers, opened dealing rooms in which the volume of business transacted increased through the 1920s and 1930s. Nevertheless, much of the international exchange dealings were still handled by the accepting houses and the branches of foreign banks.

The history of foreign exchange has been linked closely with the development of communications. In the inter-war period, telephone lines to European cities were often difficult to obtain. Sometimes it happened that one bank in London had the only available telephone line to a dealing bank in a European centre just at the time when there was a demand for, or offering of, sterling in that market. As one dealer in the room held on as long as possible to that call, other dealers in the dealing room in London would be actively trying to purchase or sell through brokers the equivalent foreign currency to other London banks who had orders from their commercial customers in that currency. As technology developed and communications throughout the world improved and became speedier, such arbitrage declined considerably.

After 1931 there followed a period of general "floating" of exchange rates, the floating being controlled to some extent by intervention, in the United Kingdom, of the "Exchange Equalisation Account" and, in wider measure, by the "Tripartite Agreement" between the United States, France and the United Kingdom, later joined by other countries.

On the outbreak of the Second World War the belligerent countries pegged their exchange rates and all transactions were executed through the central banks. The exchange markets therefore were effectively closed throughout Europe for the whole of the war period. Towards the end of the war, the Bretton Woods Conference, drawing on the experience gained between 1931 and 1938, decided the shape of the world monetary system and exchange markets for the immediate post-war years. The foreign exchange market in London re-opened at the end of 1951, but exchange regulations which controlled the free transferability of sterling slowed London's re-establishment as the world's leading foreign exchange market, as dealings were at first limited to transactions against sterling on a bilateral basis. Those controls, however, were gradually dismantled and at the end of 1958 "transferable sterling" was abolished, so that during the following years London regained its pre-eminence, albeit with some close rivals.

The free convertibility of sterling could not disguise the fact that its use as a reserve asset and trading currency was declining from the dominant position it had held as an international currency in the inter-war and immediate post-war periods. Gradually it has been superseded by the U.S. dollar, but has had competition also from the Deutschmark and the Swiss and French franc, although the governments of these countries did not wish their currencies to carry the burden and responsibilities of being reserve assets. Sterling lost its dominant position because of its weakness, causing recurrent crises and consequently loss of confidence, culminating in its devaluation in 1967. As a result of the Bretton Woods Conference, in effect all principal currencies had a fixed par value against the dollar, the dollar itself being convertible into gold. Thus, the dollar became the dominant currency in exchange markets. Currencies were allowed to fluctuate by no more than 1% either side of the par value and at these points the central banks undertook to enter the markets to buy or sell their own currency against other currencies. In the immediate post-war period these interventions were made in many currencies, as all the major countries had par values and intervention points with each other. For instance, if the French franc was offered against sterling, the Bank of England would purchase francs at its declared intervention point, and settlements were effected through the European Payments Union.

Since convertibility was established in 1958 central banks have normally had intervention points only in U.S. dollars and have mainly used that currency as a means of intervention. However, within the terms of the European "snake" (*see* page 79), intervention points in European currencies are defined and intervention in those currencies is carried out. Nowadays all international and interbank currency transactions are quoted and dealt against U.S. dollars. Thus, if a U.K. importer wishes to purchase Deutschmarks to settle an invoice, he will purchase these marks from his bank and pay the countervalue in sterling. More than likely that bank will not readily find a seller of marks against sterling, either in London or in other major dealing centres. In order to cover that sale of marks, the banks will have to purchase them against U.S. dollars and do another transaction to purchase the U.S. dollars against sterling to complete the operation.

The capital markets of the United States have played a major role in financing the development of world economies. As a result of this financing, the currency reserves of the central banks of the countries being financed increased substantially and the dollar therefore became the most widely held international reserve asset.

One of the main tenets of the Bretton Woods Agreement was that no country should indulge in competitive devaluations in order to boost its exports, but should devalue only if it could be demonstrated that there was a fundamental disequilibrium in its balance of payments. This was an attempt to create stable conditions which had been absent during the inter-war years and, it was thought at the time, would be conducive to confidence in the monetary system and consequently encourage a steady growth in the volume of world trade. Although the system evolved as a result of the Bretton Woods Conference has subsequently collapsed, it is undeniable that it did contribute to the growth of post-war trade and the rebuilding of war-damaged economies. Much later it was deficient in its ability to enforce the dollar-gold convertibility of the dollar or the revaluation of the strong currencies or to cope with the vast increase in the volume of funds circulating in the international money markets.

These liquid funds led to the creation of the Eurodollar market, the most significant development in foreign exchange markets during the last two decades. Its growth coincided with the weakness of the dollar and the emergence of a deficit in the balance of payments of the United States. This gradually worsening deficit fuelled the Eurodollar market at an increasing rate and produced huge amounts of liquid funds which could readily move across the exchanges to be converted from one currency to another. Eventually their flows became so huge that no central bank acting independently, or even in collaboration with other monetary authorities, was able to maintain continued intervention at its support rate. Sizeable interventions were usually made by central banks of the strongest currencies, partly because the U.S. Federal Reserve Bank did not hold sufficient foreign currencies, despite large and elaborate swap arrangements with other central banks and monetary authorities, to enable it to intervene effectively except on a few isolated occasions. (By swap arrangements is meant, in this context, the willingness of one central bank to accept the indebtedness of another country in exchange for a loan of the former's own currency.)

In retrospect, this was one of the weaknesses of the Bretton Woods Agreement, particularly as the dollar has in effect not been convertible into gold since the early 1960s – except for the conversion of dollars into gold by President de Gaulle in 1965. It was not until August 1971 that the United States officially suspended the convertibility of dollars into gold which eventually brought to an end the system of fixed exchange rates and the advent of floating exchanges. Following the breakdown of the parities agreed in December 1971 in Washington – the so-called Smithsonian agreement – some European countries, principally the members of the E.E.C., attempted to maintain a joint float against the U.S. dollar, and to limit the fluctuations of their currencies against each other within a relatively narrow range (the so-called "snake in the tunnel" agreement). At first, this has had only limited success, and some countries have had to leave the joint float because the weakness of their currencies brought strains to that system. Subsequently, the system was developed and adapted to include a number of additional countries and to allow for greater flexibility, but, at the time of writing, the United Kingdom remains outside the system.

In October 1979, the operation of United Kingdom exchange control was suspended, although the framework of the Act remains on the statute book.

In September 1982, the London International Financial Futures Exchange (LIFFE) opened its doors. This new market provides an alternative means of hedging movements in foreign interest rates or foreign exchange rates, although the latter may be better dealt with on the interbank market. All the accepting houses are members of LIFFE, but it is too early to indicate what impact LIFFE may make upon their business.

Functions of Foreign Exchange Dealing Rooms

It is against this background that foreign exchange dealing rooms have operated and are operating. What functions do they perform and how do they perform them? Their principal function is to service their customers who are engaged in international foreign trade and investment. Purchases and sales of foreign currencies are by no means the only service provided by banks to such customers; detailed information on markets and forecasts of the course of foreign exchange rates are frequently requested. Accepting houses have traditionally played an important role in fulfilling these requests and now all major dealing banks undertake much research to enable them to advise their customers on many of the problems arising in present-day markets, including the effects of other countries' exchange control and regulations on international business. Such advice could range from the opportunities available to cover a commitment in a foreign currency at a future date and the timing of such covering, as well as advice on the financing of international projects by borrowing in the Eurocurrency markets, and the exchange risks involved in such financing operations.

The advent of floating rates has made the task of giving such advice even more difficult than it was previously, with short-term flows of enormous amounts of funds capable of moving exchange rates by 10% in a matter of weeks. Today there are very many factors which can at any one time influence the course of the rate of exchange: balance of trade, balance of payments, interest arbitrage, rate of inflation, money supply, terms of trade, growth of gross national product, gross national product as a percentage of overseas trade, relative strength of trading partners, political stability and, more recently, the investment policies of the oil-producing countries.

Foreign exchange dealing rooms are not only executing their own customers' business but acting for their overseas correspondent banks, and for banks in their own financial centres. This is a very important function, essential to the smooth operation of the international markets.

The foreign exchange market does not exist in any specific place: it is a vast complex of telephone and telex lines joining the whole international banking community together like a spider's web with London at its centre. It is the nearest approach to a "perfect" market in the economic meaning of the word, in that the price is determined by supply and demand at any one time. Owing to the sophisticated speed of communications available today, a demand in one area of the world can be supplied from a centre in a distant area. In order to understand the structure of the exchange market, it is important to appreciate that it is a world market, and consequently it is impossible to have a situation in which one currency against another can remain at different rates in two different world financial centres for any space of time, because banks would buy in one centre and sell in the other to bring those rates into line, provided that there were no exchange control restrictions to this arbitrage and that normal means of communication were not interrupted. All banks in the world, therefore, who have any business and are authorised by their central bank to undertake foreign exchange transactions, even if they deal only in their local centre, contribute to the total volume of business in the world foreign exchange market.

Banks always deal as principals in their exchange operations, buying and selling in their own name, but London foreign exchange brokers always act as intermediaries by matching buyers and sellers. The increase in the number of broking houses (and of their staff) is indicative of the general growth of the foreign exchange market since the early 1960s. London brokers who then employed less than ten people now employ more than a hundred.

Between the two world wars the number of foreign exchange brokers in London was far in excess of that required to transact the available business. After the Second World War, it was decided that, in order to maintain a more efficient and orderly market, it would be appropriate to have a smaller number of broking firms and to group them into an association. The Foreign Exchange Brokers Association was formed in 1951 with eight member firms. It has remained independent and manages its own affairs, supervising the conduct of member brokers. Since then, in view of the increase in the volume of business, and the development of the currency deposit market, the number of brokers has increased – there are now 12 – and the Association, renamed the Foreign Exchange and Currency Deposit Brokers Association (F.E.C.D.B.A.), now includes firms which act as brokers in foreign exchange and currency deposits. The brokers are now represented world-wide and enable London banks to deal internationally even more effectively.

In 1937, on the initiative of the then Governor of the Bank of England, a Foreign Exchange Committee was formed by representatives of banks to bring some order into the market in regard to the mechanics of dealing, broking and the relationship between the banks and brokers. The Foreign Exchange Committee (incorporated into the British Bankers' Association in June 1975) continues, under the supervision of the Bank of England, to ensure that an orderly market in foreign exchange and currency deposits is maintained in London. The Bank, taking into account any representations made by the Foreign Exchange Committee, fixes the scale of brokerage applicable to deals in the London market between banks and recognised brokers and makes its views on matters relating to the market known to a joint standing committee of the banks and the brokers.

The many hundreds of banks actively engaged throughout the world in foreign exchange business have enabled the world's trading companies to cover their commitments, however huge, quickly and efficiently. One of the chief fears about the system of floating rates was that its introduction would make it impossible for firms engaged in international trade to estimate their risks or cover their commitments, but this has not been realised because, in fact, the forward market has remained active and viable and has provided adequate means of covering future exchange risks at reasonable cost.

There is little doubt that one of the most essential services in foreign exchange which banks provide for their customers and correspondent banks is the maintenance of a fluid forward market. Their ability to do so depends principally on the degree of sophistication of the domestic money markets in the countries of the relevant currencies. The course of forward rates depends on the differential between the rates of interest in the money markets of the two currencies. Interest rate arbitrage soon corrects any temporary distortion in the forward exchange rates. It follows, therefore, that the most active and sophisticated forward market is that for sterling against the dollar, which probably accounts for around one-half of all forward dealings in London. Many accepting houses have been very active and, due to the close collaboration which their sterling money market dealers have had with their foreign exchange dealers, have been able to operate very successfully in this market, for both short and long periods – even up to five years.

It is usual practice for banks operating internationally in foreign exchange, both spot and forward, to hold positions for short periods in order to provide a fluid market enabling them to give competitive rates to their customers.

However, events in 1974 in West Germany, where losses were caused by the time differences between banking houses in different hemispheres, have caused banks to make a reassessment of the risks inherent in foreign exchange trading and the financial control of these operations has become subject to very strict reporting. Nowadays, this type of financial control increasingly involves the use of sophisticated computerised systems.

In fact, of course, the management of accepting houses has traditionally been closely involved in the day-to-day running of dealing rooms because, when these banks were family partnerships, the senior partner was in many cases also the principal dealer. By and large, such a tradition is continued and even in larger organisations such as the clearing banks, the senior management of the overseas branch would be fully informed of the dealing activities of the bank.

With strong competition from large domestic and foreign banks, the proportion of the volume of business handled by accepting houses has declined, and in order to maintain their present position they will need to call upon their distinctive qualities, namely flexibility, adaptability, inventiveness and the ability to reach quick decisions. As these qualities do emerge strongly in the face of competition, the members of the Accepting Houses Committee should be assured in the future of a significant role in the London foreign exchange market.

12

THE MANAGEMENT OF THE BALANCE SHEET, AND DEPOSITS AND LOANS

The day-to-day banking business of a merchant bank comprises typically the provision of loans made on a medium- and short-term basis in addition to money market activities in both foreign currency and sterling, together with foreign exchange business. This entails sophisticated management of the bank's balance sheet, since if the lending business of a merchant bank is directed towards the creation of attractive assets, the management of the liability structure of the balance sheet is of paramount importance to the stability and financial health of the institution. In the case of an accepting house, the management of its liability structure is, perhaps, a particularly sensitive determinant of its profitability and long-term prosperity, since it has to pay interest on virtually all its deposits. The accepting house differs from its clearing bank counterpart, as it does not enjoy the benefit of an extensive branch network throughout the country from which a significant percentage of funds could be derived in the form of non-interest or low interest-bearing current accounts.

The growth of banking business in London in the 1970s, as illustrated by the rapid expansion of balance sheets, was partly due to continuous growth of the sterling market, but more importantly to that of Eurocurrency business as a result of London's predominant position in the Eurocurrency markets. Whereas the growth of currency deposits in London was principally a feature of the activities of the overseas banks, in particular during the late 1970s of the U.S. and Japanese banks, the accepting houses also shared in the expansion of the Eurocurrency business generally. Thus, by August 1982 currency deposits accounted for around 60% of the accepting houses' deposit base, against 51% in 1972. At the same time, however, it has to be recognised that the importance of the accepting houses as banking institutions when measured by size of balance sheet has diminished over the years in comparison with the expansion of their commercial counterparts. The share of the accepting houses in total deposits of banks in the United Kingdom fell from over 5% (£4.8 billion) in December 1974 to around 3.5% (£16.6 billion) in August 1982 (*see* Table 12.1).

Bank of England Supervision

A principal factor which has supported London's position as the world's major Eurocurrency centre has been the relatively liberal attitude of the Bank of England towards the supervision of banks operating in London. During a ten-year period of rapid expansion in the international banking markets, which has been accompanied by intervals of volatility as a result of fluctuations in currencies and interest rates and more recently of increased credit risk, the Bank of England has desisted from the imposition of restrictive regulations to govern the operation of banks in London. While recognising the fundamental need for protection for depositors in addition to its intermediary role of sustaining economic activity with the maintenance of a sound banking system, the Bank of England had adopted a flexible approach towards banking supervision, with a high degree of reliance on regular communication with the management of individual institutions.

Inevitably, as a result of the secondary banking crisis in 1974 and developments in the international banking community as a whole, this supervision has been widened beyond its original scope and the *Banking Act, 1979* has vested in the Bank of England statutory responsibility for the supervision of deposit-taking institutions. The *Banking Act* seeks to regulate the acceptance of deposits by institutions in the course of deposit-taking business and confers upon the Bank of England certain functions with respect to the control of these institutions. The Act provides for the Bank of England to grant recognised bank status to selected institutions, subject to their satisfying certain criteria (as defined in the Act) with particular regard to financial standing and management. As a second tier, the Bank of England is also empowered to grant licensed deposit-taker status to other

Table 12.1 Deposits of U.K. Banks (£ billions)

	Dec 1972		Dec 1974		Dec 1977		Dec 1980		Aug 1982	
	£	Currency	£	Currency	£	Currency	£	Currency	£	Currency
Clearing banks	16.73	2.63	25.14	3.72	31.21	6.26	48.35	13.18	64.66	24.81
Accepting houses	2.09	2.19	2.16	2.65	3.31	3.64	5.29	6.18	6.80	9.81
Overseas banks	6.51	28.62	8.86	54.79	10.73	90.21	18.90	141.99	24.82	261.90
Other U.K. banks (consortium banks, etc.)	5.43	2.88	7.54	4.58	11.24	20.59	17.79	32.12	30.24	51.69
Totals	30.76	36.32	43.70	65.74	56.49	120.70	90.33	193.47	126.52	348.21

institutions which are able only to meet more limited criteria than those required for recognised bank status. All accepting houses enjoy recognised bank status and are thus able to operate with almost complete freedom in the taking of sterling and currency deposits or the making of loans on a day-to-day basis.

In the execution of the Bank's statutory responsibilities, the Bank encourages banks to pursue prudent internal controls over balance sheet structure. The Bank has focused on three major factors to which guidelines are applied: first, the adequacy of the capital base (measured by total assets to free capital and reserves, and a risk/asset ratio with weighting applied to different classes of assets); secondly, a liquidity ratio (measured by the maturity profile of the assets and liabilities comprising the balance sheet); and, thirdly, foreign exchange limits (measured by the magnitude of currency positions).

Liquidity

The various measurements described above are closely related, although it is perhaps the liquidity ratio which is most subject to daily fluctuation and which demands particular attention from those responsible for the management of a bank's balance sheet. Since the whole basis of banking is the borrowing of short-term and the lending of longer-term money, it is of fundamental importance to any bank that it be able to meet from its liquid assets the proportion of its current liabilities which is likely to be called upon, given possible market circumstances. In the case of a clearing bank, liquidity is ultimately dictated by the need to be able to repay sight deposits (current account balances), of which only a small proportion are likely to be withdrawn at any given time, and traditionally the clearing banks have maintained a liquidity ratio of roughly 30%. An accepting house is in a different position, owing to the different composition of its liabilities, and it needs to maintain a higher liquidity ratio than a clearing bank, with 40 to 50% being quite normal.

Structure of the Balance Sheet

Set out in Table 12.2 is a summary balance sheet for a fictitious, but perhaps typical, accepting house.

Deposits

The principal difference between the liability side of this balance

Table 12.2 A Summary Balance Sheet for an Accepting House (£ millions)

Share capital and reserves		*Current assets*	
Issued share capital	25	Balances with banks, money at call and at short notice and bullion	240
Reserves	35	Bank certificates of deposit and bills discounted	75
		Government and local authority listed securities	15
Current liabilities and provisions		Other loans to banks and local authorities	265
Current deposit and other accounts, including inner reserves and provision for taxation	930		
Other	35	*Advances and other accounts*	
		Loans, advances and other accounts	355
		Assets held for leasing	25
		Other	10
		Investments and fixed assets	
		Investments in subsidiaries and associates	10
		Other investments and securities held	25
		Property, plant and equipment and other fixed assets	5
Acceptances on behalf of customers	175	*Liability of customers for acceptances*	175
	1,200		1,200

sheet and that of a clearing bank's balance sheet is the ratio of deposits from customers to deposits from banks. In the case of our typical accepting house this ratio is 2 or 3:1, whereas for a clearing bank it might be as high as 7:1. The accepting house, which deals normally with relatively large depositors in one or perhaps two branches, does not in general have access to the large sums which (in aggregate) individuals place with the clearing banks, and its "customer base" normally consists of large industrial and commercial companies, institutions and wealthy private individuals. These funds, sometimes called "natural deposits", are obtained by accepting houses at rates generally above those offered to individuals by clearing banks, but, as explained below, they normally represent the most attractive form of funding to an accepting house.

An accepting house will supplement these natural deposits by bidding for deposits from other banks in the interbank market, often using money brokers. Funds raised from other banks will normally be more expensive than natural deposits and it is this source of funds which represents the houses' marginal cost of raising funds. An accepting house will try to maximise the amount derived from the natural or direct type of deposit by building up a clientèle both in the United Kingdom and abroad on which it can rely to deposit a certain volume of funds. It will depend as little as possible on the interbank or indirect type, partly because deposits from customers are likely to be cheaper, but also because an undue reliance on the indirect source can result in volatility in times of confused or delicate market conditions. Every bank normally sets a limit on the amount of funds which it is prepared to place with any other bank, according to the size and standing of the latter, and thus any "bidder" for deposits must recognise that its capacity as a borrower in the interbank market is ultimately limited. A broad range of potential direct depositors is a fundamental basis for a sound banking business.

Just as most deposits with accepting houses bear interest, so they are largely of a "time" nature rather than a "sight" nature. The period for which individual deposits are obtained will normally reflect the depositor's wishes. The rate of interest paid, while to some extent subject to negotiation with the depositor, will broadly correspond to the "market" rate at the time for the relevant period. By adjusting the rates he quotes, the chief dealer, (*see* page 93), whose function it is to run the "book", will endeavour, and may be able, to tailor the period of a direct deposit to suit the book. Where he draws on the interbank or indirect market, he can normally obtain a deposit for the period he requires, subject, of course, to any limits on his borrowing capacity and to the state of the market's confidence generally.

Where foreign currency deposits are concerned, the dealer will normally have the choice, when dealing in the interbank market, either to take a deposit in the currency required or to "create" the deposit by taking in another currency and "swapping" it into the currency he needs. Funds in currencies other than the U.S. dollar form only a relatively small part of the total Eurocurrency market (20 to 25% of the total of U.S. $1,900 billion in mid 1982) and a dollar deposit transformed by a "swap" may be more convenient and sometimes even cheaper than a straight deposit in the other currency. In such instances, the deposit and foreign exchange dealers must work closely together.

The maturity of individual deposits varies and the dealer will have in his book and will seek to maintain, as a reflection of the way in which he employs the funds, a spread of maturities ranging from call (that is, capable of being demanded from the borrower) to, say, five years, with the bulk typically in periods of less than three months.

Certificates of Deposit (and other instruments)

Although deposits represent the principal source of funding for a bank's assets, additional funding can be obtained from its issue of marketable paper. The main instrument used is the certificate of deposit, which is a form of transferable bank deposit. The holders of these instruments include other banks, discount houses and large companies and institutions with surplus funds. The certificate of deposit (C.D.) was introduced into London in the mid 1960s and the development of the market in these instruments can be seen from Table 12.3.

Although the accepting houses' principal role in this market is as holders of other banks' C.D.s, they also issue these instruments themselves, usually in sterling or U.S. dollars, as a means of funding. In mid August 1982, the volume of outstanding C.D.s issued by accepting houses amounted to £636 million (of which roughly two-thirds were denominated in sterling).

There are several other instruments (such as floating rate notes) which are used by banks as a means of raising further funds, but these normally result in a funding cost higher than that obtainable in the interbank market. For this reason, and because of the

Table 12.3 Volume of Certificates of Deposit
Issued by Banks in the U.K. (£ millions)

	Sterling	Currency
Dec 1966	–	80
Dec 1969	442	1,541
Dec 1972	4,926	3,072
Dec 1978	3,809	14,132
Dec 1979	3,833	19,775
Dec 1980	5,727	20,946
Dec 1981	6,695	40,424
Aug 1982	8,440	55,237

relatively restrictive internal controls which accepting houses set on the expansion of their balance sheets, the accepting houses have not yet followed the international banks into these other markets. The prices at which all these instruments (including C.D.s) trade are subject to considerable fluctuation, particularly in times of difficult market conditions, such as those in the U.K. following the secondary banking crisis in 1973/74 and in many parts of the world in 1982, and it is consistent with the cautious approach of the accepting houses that they have hitherto avoided the necessity of raising large amounts in this way.

Bank of England Deposit Requirements

Under provisions introduced in August 1981 to replace the monetary control system known as "competition and credit control" which was established a decade earlier, the Bank of England requires all recognised banks and licensed deposit-takers to deposit ½% of their eligible liabilities with the Bank in the form of non-interest-bearing deposits. A further requirement, applying only to eligible banks, is for such banks to maintain call deposits with the discount houses amounting on average to 6% of eligible liabilities. Furthermore, banks and licensed deposit-takers may from time to time be required to place "special deposits" with the Bank as a means of controlling the money supply.

These provisions result in a cost to the banks arising from, first, the loss of interest on those deposits required to be kept with the Bank of England, and, secondly, the shortfall between the yield obtainable on call deposits with the discount houses and that ruling on other market assets. These costs currently amount to approximately ³/₁₆% per annum and, given the low level of margins obtainable on most banking assets (few of which yield

more than 1% above the cost of funds to banks), it is usual for them
to be passed on to the customer. A provision to cover variations in
the calculation of these costs (and in the basis of the Bank of
England's requirements) has become standard in sterling loan
agreements.

Asset Management

Liquid Assets

The structure of an accepting house's deposits and other liabilities, and its self-imposed prudential ratios, will have an
important influence on its lending activities. As a general rule, an
accepting house will always try to maintain a relatively high ratio
of liquid assets to current liabilities. These liquid assets are defined
as balances with banks and money at call, U.K. Treasury bills,
certificates of deposit, bills discounted and money at short notice
with a maximum maturity of seven days.

The accepting houses' most flexible liquid assets, call loans to
the London discount market, have a particular significance in that
the discount market is an essential element in the mechanism of
the acceptance credit (the original basis of the accepting houses'
banking business). The system of monetary control established by
the Bank of England in 1981 (see above), provides for the
maintenance with the discount market of a certain proportion of
any eligible bank's volume of their "eligible liabilities" (a term
defined by the Bank and broadly equal to the excess of inward
sterling deposits over outward sterling deposits with other
financial institutions) in the form of call loans. Since the discount
market has direct access to the Bank of England as lender of last
resort, such call loans are the first line of liquidity available to any
bank.

Uncommitted Facilities

Accepting houses frequently make available short-term finance to
their corporate customers in the form of uncommitted lines of
credit. These are provided by way of facilities under which a
customer may from time to time draw loans up to a certain
maximum amount, subject to mutual agreement with the lender
on each occasion. If the bank finds it unattractive to make such a
loan available on a particular day (for example, because its
prudential ratios are close to their maximum levels), it will have
the option to decline to do so – even though the position may well

be reversed within a matter of days. Such arrangements are normally only of interest to large corporate customers, who will often have a large number of uncommitted lines in place from a broad spread of banks from which they will seek the most competitive funds. The costs of arranging such facilities are normally minimal and the documentation simple and so far as the bank is concerned the asset is short term.

Rollover Loans

While maintaining a relatively high liquidity ratio, an accepting house will wish to undertake an adequate volume of medium-term lending business in order to satisfy the requirements of its clients (as well as benefiting from the more attractive returns on these longer-term commitments).

As we have seen, the bulk of funds deposited with banks is for periods of less than three months. These deposits carry a fixed rate of interest until their maturity. At maturity, the bank has to go back into the interbank market (or seek further direct deposits) to maintain the funding of its portfolio of assets. Market interest rates are subject to considerable fluctuation and, in order to protect the profit on a transaction (*i.e.* the margin), the accepting houses (in common with most other banks) accordingly relate their lending interest rates directly to the cost of borrowing from other banks in the interbank market. The basic rate used as a reference point is the London interbank offered rate (LIBOR) for the period and currency in question. LIBOR is a floating interest rate, subject to continual fluctuations. The frequency of rate fixing is normally one, two, three or six monthly and the provision of loans on a committed basis for periods longer than six months will therefore entail adjustments to the interest rate to accommodate the cost of new deposits. These regular extensions are known as "rollovers".

Duties of the Chief Dealer

The sources of an accepting house's deposits, some of the uses to which they are put and the fundamental importance of liquidity have been considered, but these will form a basis for profitable activity only if the chief dealer judges future movements in interest rates correctly. Leaving other considerations aside, it is clear that when interest rates are rising he should be fixing his deposits for a longer period than those for which he is lending, while a falling market will encourage him to take in short-term deposits and make longer-term loans. Even within the compass of a day's business the right judgement as to short-term fluctuations can make the difference between a profit and a loss. The chief dealer must have constant regard to the liquidity requirements of the bank, and will thus be constrained in maximising his gain or minimising his loss from a movement in interest rates.

The essence of money management can best be summed up in terms of the chief dealer's principal tasks, which are fourfold:

(a) to accept and seek deposits from customers;
(b) to ensure the bank's ability to repay such deposits by applying the liquidity policy laid down by his management;
(c) to secure the requisite funds for the bank's loan portfolio by obtaining further deposits from either customers or banks;
(d) to arrange the maturities within the criteria of the liquidity policy so as to maximise the return on the capital employed to support the deposit base of the bank.

As an integral part of the duties set out above, the chief dealer will develop and foster good relations with a wide variety of customers, banks and brokers, and will, if required, provide an advisory service to customers on the employment of liquid funds. The increased level of interest rates in recent years has acted as an incentive to corporate treasurers to pay greater attention to the flow of their companies' funds. Indeed, many of the principles described above apply equally to the management of such funds. This has led to increasing reliance on advice from accepting houses and to a corresponding development of the service offered. The parallel development of the need for advice on exchange risks has also involved chief foreign exchange dealers in a similar and equally important function. This service goes well beyond the pure functions of seeking deposits and the advice given may even result in funds being placed elsewhere.

The chief dealer of an accepting house, whether in deposits or in foreign exchange, is thus in many ways a highly important point of contact, not only with the market, but also with customers and the bank's relations with customers may often turn on his skill and diplomacy.

PART FOUR

OTHER SERVICES
OF THE ACCEPTING HOUSES

13

INVESTMENT MANAGEMENT ACTIVITIES

During the course of the 1970s, the accepting houses emerged as a major force in the business of investment management. This arose partly from the continuation of the significant growth of the size and coverage of funded pension schemes, a speciality of the accepting houses, and partly from the demand for international portfolio management services.

This latter seems to have followed the growth in world trade, the instability of currencies following the floating of the U.S. dollar in 1971 and the emergence of the OPEC surpluses arising from the oil price increases of 1973 and 1978. The suspension of U.K. exchange controls in October 1979 provided a major additional impetus to demand from U.K. resident investors.

There are no published figures of the total value of investment funds under the direct management of the accepting houses, but it is unlikely to be less than £20,000 million. Many of the directors and staff are involved with pension funds, insurance companies, investment trusts, charities, educational foundations, local authorities, foreign government financial agencies, etc., as directors of such bodies, as members of investment committees or as advisers. This spreads the influence of the accepting houses well beyond portfolios directly under their control. On average some 20% of the staff employed by accepting houses is concerned with investment matters.

The investment management operations of the accepting houses are unique in the financial world for the level of sophistication and geographical diversity of their skills. The reasons for this are twofold: first, the intimate involvement of accepting houses in the complex web of financial and other markets throughout the world and, second, the international nature of the development of British capitalism in the last 150 years.

The return in the 1960s and 1970s to a much greater involvement in international finance by the accepting houses has resulted in many of the leading houses opening representative offices, subsidiaries or joint ventures in a large number of the world's financial centres. Many of these operations conduct investment management business and all are, of course, listening posts for the investment decisions of the houses in London. The most important overseas centres are New York, Frankfurt, Paris, Tokyo, Zürich, Geneva, Singapore and Hong Kong.

Regulation

Mention is made in Appendix C of the important, even vital, separation of the corporate finance divisions of the merchant banks from their investment divisions, thus ensuring that no privileged information is used in forming investment policy. There has also been over the years a gradual build-up of political pressure to strengthen and formalise, among other things, the regulations surrounding the conduct of investment management. Following the publication of the Gower Report in January 1982, it is possible that a regulatory body or bodies will be set up to ensure that the high standards common to the accepting houses will be adopted by all those who have the responsibility of investing other people's money.

Development of Investment Management Services

Involvement in investment management activities probably stems from a combination of historic accident and a traditional ability to adapt available skills to a constantly changing environment. Its genesis was in the deployment of the large fortunes made by some of the Victorian merchant bankers. It developed with the handling of the investments of their trading clients and of their moneyed friends. The first major experience of handling public funds came with the short-lived investment trust boom of the late 1920s.

Until the 1950s, the techniques of investment management, although often successful, were somewhat unsophisticated and relied rather upon long-accepted rules of investment based on the soundness of fixed interest securities, particularly government stocks. Few of the houses had many specialist investment staff or, indeed, a specific investment division. Portfolios were often in the care of partners or directors who had many other banking or corporate responsibilities.

By the mid 1950s, a number of important social and economic developments had taken place. Perhaps the most important was that inflation, albeit at low rates, had secured a firm foothold. At the same time, the sources of savings and capital had become much more widely spread and savings were beginning to move from the traditional safe havens of savings banks, building societies, etc., into the more inflation-proofed unit trusts and with-profits life policies.

The collective responsibility philosophy of the post-war Welfare State and the provisions of the Taxes Acts allowing superannuation contributions to accumulate free of tax were two of the causes of a rapid growth in the number and coverage of pension funds, once the prerogative of the Civil Service, white-collar staff and the professions.

The accepting houses reacted quickly to the considerable increase in the flow of capital available for investment arising from many sources. They rapidly built on their existing skills and knowledge to deal efficiently both with the increased volume of capital arising from these new sources of savings and also in recent years, with the greater complexity of the financial and political world, which makes investment judgements increasingly difficult.

As time, taxation and social change have taken their toll of large personal fortunes, the importance to the accepting houses of the management of private portfolios has diminished to make way for the newer forms of aggregation of capital.

Investment trusts, although to a degree superseded by unit trusts as the small saver's means of access to professional investment management, still number over 200 with net assets of £8.2 billion and total market capitalisation of £6 billion, which represents about 5% of the value of quoted securities on The Stock Exchange. The accepting houses manage 39 of these investment trusts.

The accepting houses also entered into the field of unit trust management some years ago. This was for two main reasons: the recognition of a wide source of new savings from the small investor who otherwise would find it difficult to get access to the investment expertise available in the accepting houses and also the need to solve the problem of existing personal portfolios whose size does not justify a full portfolio management service. Many accepting houses offer a wide range of unit trusts for different investment purposes, but generally they do not enter into the more speculative areas of investment and tend to concentrate on the more solidly based "blue chip" growth companies, together with quite high exposure to investment in overseas stock markets.

The leading position of the accepting houses in the management of the assets of self-administered pension funds has been established for some years. This may be regarded as a natural extension of the financial services offered to U.K. companies and public sector bodies.

As a result of the quality of the investment management service which the accepting houses and others are able to offer, more companies, large and small, are moving from insured pension schemes to self-administered schemes. Companies are also abandoning the practice of themselves managing their pension fund portfolios.

Many funds adopted the U.S. practice of splitting their pension fund between different houses. A number of houses have also extended their pension fund service into the field of actuarial and advisory services.

In recent years the source and variety of clients from outside the U.K. has grown and widened – governments and central banks, international agencies, offshore insurance companies, European, North American and offshore pension funds and many others. In order to meet this challenge many of the skills which were previously only of peripheral importance to the investment process have become central to the proper management of the assets of these clients. These skills include interest rate and currency judgements, sovereign and corporate risk analysis and a knowledge of all the major equity, fixed interest and money markets around the world. Equity investment analysis has also become a far more complex discipline. Organisations with large sums of capital in their care are expected to be able to comprehend and judge the risk and return factors in such diverse and complicated fields as biotechnology, telecommunications and oil and gas exploration.

It should be noted with some satisfaction that many of these developments, both in the source of clients and the nature of the investments made, has brought the accepting houses into direct and successful competition with the world's leading investment institutions.

Organisation of Investment Management Services

Some 25 years ago most of the tasks related to the management of a portfolio were usually conducted by one individual. The increasing complexity of the decisions required of a portfolio manager has resulted in a growth of specialisation within investment management organisations. The process seems very likely to continue. Notwithstanding this, the portfolio manager, with his ultimate responsibility to the house's clients for the management of their assets, remains the key central figure in the organisation. *De facto*, he may delegate many decisions and responsibilities to research analysts, foreign market specialists, currency experts, property managers, etc., but it is he who will face the client with the overall result of the house's stewardship.

14

AUTOMATED REAL-TIME INVESTMENTS EXCHANGE LIMITED (ARIEL)

Origin of ARIEL

ARIEL (short for Automated Real-time Investments Exchange Ltd) was established in 1972 and its entire capital was at the outset held by all the members of the Accepting Houses Committee (then 17 in number) in proportions roughly corresponding to the amount of investment business commanded by them, subject to a maximum of 10% and a minimum of 1% for any one holder. As the result of a re-organisation in 1980 the capital is now held by 11 merchant banks and seven insurance companies.

The background to ARIEL is interesting. It was in the early 1970s that the accepting houses realised that, with the huge expansion in dealing in equities that was taking place and in which they were major participants, they were collectively paying very large sums indeed in commission to stockbrokers; it was known that several were paying more than £1 million annually in such commissions. Valuable though brokers' services unquestionably are – in execution, in research, in "after-care" – some houses, and perhaps especially those with their own research departments, felt that they were paying too much for those services. At the same time, the increasing importance of the institutions and the sheer size of their dealings were putting severe strains on the jobbing system's ability to cope, and the market's "liquidity", at times, was not all that could reasonably be desired. It was these factors that mainly concentrated the minds of the accepting houses on the possibility of developing a computer-based block trading system suitable for large-scale dealing in U.K. and other securities directly and cheaply between institutional investors, both inside the United Kingdom and possibly, as time went by, throughout Europe.

A visit to the United States in the autumn of 1971 by a "Specialists' Subcommittee" of the Accepting Houses Committee was instrumental in showing just how great were the advances in the dissemination of information about securities which computer-based technology had made possible. Admittedly, most of the systems in existence were basically sophisticated information systems, designed to enhance the level of trading through the normal channels. ARIEL was, however, developed along the lines of an institutional dealing system called INSTINET (based in New York) with which ARIEL came to an arrangement as to the acquisition of know-how.

ARIEL was established in 1972 as a computer-based block trading system in securities for U.K. institutions. The ARIEL system went "live" in February 1974 with, at that time, 25 subscribers: this number steadily increased over the next two years to over 60, including a majority of the United Kingdom's leading investment institutions. Moreover, one objective of ARIEL was achieved even before it went "live" in that, in response to what it believed to be the competitive threat of ARIEL, The Stock Exchange cut its own commissions drastically, especially for large bargains in equities.

In its conception ARIEL was designed to be a computer-based operation, deals occurring only through ARIEL's central computer between subscribers, each of whom had a terminal. Each of the terminals consisted of a screen, an associated printer and a keyboard and they were connected by private Post Office line to the central computer, situated in ARIEL's offices.

The central computer kept a "book" for each security in the system into which subscribers might enter their buying and selling interests, which were normally broadcast to all other subscribers. These "books" could be searched to see what entries there were on the "other side". From this information or through broadcasts, negotiations could take place privately and anonymously via the central computer. When a bargain was struck by one subscriber accepting a "bid" or "offer" of another, a detailed record of the bargain was displayed on the screens and printers of both parties.

It was also possible to call up information on any security in the system, *e.g.* the current price range of both buyers and sellers, the aggregate volume and price range of bargains made in the current

month and preceding month, and the size and price of each of the
last four bargains executed on the system.

Developments in ARIEL

Despite a successful launch and support for ARIEL from most of
the accepting houses, and despite the assistance of a substantial
volume of "bed-and-breakfast" business flowing through ARIEL,
its use by subscribers from 1976 gradually dwindled until by 1982
the number of subscribers had fallen back to about 25, the number
with which ARIEL had started. This decline may be attributed to
several factors: the stock market collapse in equity shares of 1974;
the fact that ARIEL was precluded by the Bank of England from
dealing in gilt-edged securities which then provided the main
active market; the limitations and imperfections of a machine-
based system; or a disinclination on the part of dealers to deal
through a machine rather than a human being; or a combination of
some or all of these factors. The experience of 1982 suggests that
the last two factors were the most important.

It became plain that dealers, *i.e.* those in subscribers' offices
with a terminal at their elbow, nevertheless preferred to pick up
the telephone and negotiate or communicate through ARIEL by
that means as to what shares they were interested in buying or
selling, at what price and in what volume. Accordingly the use
of the terminal was progressively phased out as subscribers
discontinued its use and the telephone has superseded it. A
central computer (a 1981 mini-computer) remains in ARIEL's
offices, together with the stock of terminals, so that the viability of
a computer-based operation still exists, but subscribers no longer
pay a rent and the circle of ARIEL users has been extended to a
number of professional institutional investors of undoubted
credit. With these developments, ARIEL's business, which had
been on the decline for some years, increased markedly, so that
ARIEL is now trading at a profit.

Advantages of ARIEL

It was, and is, a central feature of ARIEL that those who use its
facilities do so on an anonymous and confidential basis. ARIEL
acts simply as agent for the vendor and for the purchaser (on the
basis of a "master" written agreement between ARIEL and its
users), in matching a bargain at a common negotiated price. For its

services ARIEL charges the parties a commission in accordance with its published commission scale, which is materially lower than that of The Stock Exchange. In addition, there is no jobbers' "turn". Thus, the costs of dealing on ARIEL are materially less than those of dealing on The Stock Exchange.

However, ARIEL has never been intended to "replace" The Stock Exchange or to be a substitute for it. Rather, it was set up purely as an alternative market place – one which offers anonymity, cheapness and (on occasion) liquidity – as opposed to, say, market information or research. Viewed as a specialised kind of broker – and ARIEL has roughly the turnover size of a medium-sized firm of stockbrokers – it can perhaps be seen in a less threatening context. To the merchant banker employed in the investment department of a bank, ARIEL's relevance lies in its existence as a supplemental market facility, which alone prevents The Stock Exchange from constituting a monopoly.

15

LEASING

Leasing is not a new business: indeed, ship chartering – a form of leasing – was known in the days of the ancient world. Contracts have been discovered inscribed on clay tablets.

In the early 1960s facilities for leasing industrial equipment first started to become widely available in the United Kingdom. The form of these facilities followed that used in the United States, where they had been available for some years previously. However, it was not until the early 1970s, when the current system of taxation with tax-based benefit investment incentives was introduced, that leasing established itself as a major source of finance. Within a very short time first-year allowances for plant and machinery were at a rate of 100% of the cost of the asset, which proved to be a very valuable incentive, but only if the investor had sufficient taxable profits to absorb the allowances. Leasing introduced a method of finance which enabled companies to take advantage of these incentives even if they did not have available profits. Among the earliest companies to offer leasing facilities were a number of accepting houses. Since that time the involvement of the accepting houses in leasing has steadily expanded and developed, and during the period, as might have been expected, certain houses have developed new techniques of leasing which have been adopted widely throughout the world. It is of interest to examine the various roles the houses now play in leasing and the nature of the facilities offered. However, before this can be done, it is necessary to define what is meant by "leasing" and to establish the reasons why houses have become involved so extensively in it.

Leasing Terminology

The facilities now available are complex and varied and the leasing business has its own jargon. Leasing, renting or hiring are similar facilities in so far as one party takes goods on hire from another. Leasing, however, has been defined as follows:

A lease is a contract between a lessor, who gives on hire, and a lessee, who takes on hire, a specific asset selected from a manufacturer or vendor of such assets by the lessee. The lessor remains at all times the owner of the asset but the lessee has the possession and use of it for a period on payment of specified rentals.

Certain leases – usually referred to as "finance" or "full payout" leases – are leasing contracts written on terms which provide that the lessee must pay a minimum number of rentals which are non-cancellable during what is usually called the "primary period". These rentals are sufficient in total to amortise the lessor's capital outlay in purchasing the asset, cover the lessor's interest and taxation payment, less tax savings generated by claiming a first-year allowance and interest income from surplus funds, and provide the lessor with a return on its investment in the lease. The lessee always assumes the liability to maintain the equip-ment. This type of lease is that most commonly offered by accepting houses which lease and the principal equipment leasing companies.

Where the asset is not fully amortised during the period for which the lessee takes it on hire, the lease is usually described as an "operating lease" or a "rental contract". Sometimes a lessor may remain liable to maintain the leased equipment.

Industrial lessors are not normally dealers in secondhand equipment and it therefore follows that the bulk of their business is full payout finance leasing. Operating leases are usually granted by specialist companies, such as computer lessors, plant or contract vehicle hirers and typewriter and television rental companies.

Scope of Facilities

Leasing is used to finance a broad range of equipment, from office furniture, mini-computers, plant and machinery, to ships, aircraft and process plants. The smaller end of the market tends to be catered for by the leasing arms of the finance houses which offer this service through their branch networks throughout the U.K.

Medium and big ticket transactions are written by banks and individual lessors, who frequently employ banks to manage their leasing activities. In the case of very large transactions, a syndicate of lessors may be formed, with each lessor providing a part of the total finance. It is interesting to note that the market has developed to such an extent that now the large lessors may take individual leases for assets costing in excess of £75 million on their own books rather than syndicating the lease.

With one or two exceptions the accepting houses are engaged in the more complex leases, which frequently involve big ticket transactions, where the lease is syndicated. Compared to the clearing bank leasing subsidiaries, the accepting houses have a limited supply of taxable capacity and therefore do not have resources necessary to write very large transactions on their own. Many of the accepting houses act as lessor managers for industrial clients and therefore have this additional source of taxable capacity.

As might be expected, the average periods over which leases are granted vary according to the nature of the equipment and its cost. Low-value goods are usually leased over quite short periods up to, say, five years. The "primary period" most frequently used is five or seven years, but very high-value goods may be leased in certain special circumstances over periods as long as 15 years and longer has been known. Most lessors consider it prudent practice not to lease equipment for a primary period exceeding its foreseeable useful life and indeed they prefer usually to let it on full payout terms for less than this period.

At the expiry of the primary period the lessee will usually have the option to continue leasing the asset for a secondary period at a peppercorn rental which is generally paid annually in advance or to dispose of the equipment. In most cases the lessee is appointed the lessor's agent for the sale and is entitled to a rebate of rentals equivalent to the majority of the net sale proceeds.

Reasons for Interest of Accepting Houses in Leasing

The reasons why the accepting houses have taken such an interest in leasing as a facility are numerous, but there are three main reasons.

First, leasing is complementary to the range of other facilities available from the average accepting house. Therefore the house which offers leasing facilities broadens the base of its operations.

Contact with new leasing customers can often be developed by the house concerned and other services available from that house may later be utilised by the customer.

The second main attraction is that a house purchasing equipment for leasing to a customer is able to claim certain allowances as a consequence of its purchase of the asset, which it may set against its liability to pay tax on income. This can result in deferment of tax, which is both necessary to the profitability of the lease and beneficial to the cash flow of the house. This is more particularly described in the section on taxes below.

Thirdly, leasing as a business can be profitable from the standpoint both of the lessor and of the lending banker when he is lending to a lessor. Houses can invest their own funds at an attractive return or they can lend funds to specialist leasing companies at interest.

Tax Position of Lessor and Lessee

The fiscal positions of lessor and lessee are of importance. Under the terms of a finance lease in the U.K., legal title to the asset remains with the lessor, although the lessee has economic use of the asset. The lessor cannot grant the lessee an option to purchase the asset at the end of the lease period without forfeiting its ability to claim the tax allowances generated by its expenditure on the leased asset. The benefit to the lessor's cash flow derived from the tax allowances is fundamental to the calculation of rentals. As the leasing market has developed both in size and competitiveness, lessors have passed most of the benefit of allowances on to lessees by way of lower rental charges. These allowances may be offset against taxable income from other sources within the lessor company or by way of group relief against profits of other members of the lessor's group, provided the ownership structure is appropriate.

A standard feature of most lease agreements now is a tax variation clause which allows the lessor to vary the rentals up or down to maintain its rate of return in the event that the lessor's expenditure does not qualify for a first-year allowance or the rate of corporation tax varies during the primary period. These clauses will not, however, protect the lessor if, for example, it cannot obtain the benefit of tax allowances because of a miscalculation in the amount of taxable capacity available. It is therefore imperative that lessors monitor their tax position closely. Unless a lessor can claim allowances at the earliest opportunity it will usually mean that its return from the lease may be eroded either partially or completely.

The *Finance Act*, 1980 introduced the concept of "qualifying purpose", which means broadly that a lessor is only able to claim a first-year allowance where the lessee is liable to corporation tax on a trade within the U.K., and that for non-taxable entities, such as local authorities, a lessor is entitled only to a writing down allowance.

So far as the lessee is concerned, rentals payable in respect of leased equipment are currently wholly allowable as a business expense.

Regional Development Grants

Regional development grants and similar government cash grants may be claimed by lessors where the equipment to be leased is located in a qualifying area and the overall project of which the equipment forms a part is eligible for this form of assistance. In such circumstances the receipt of a grant by the lessor may either be reflected in the rental charged to the lessee or grossed up at the current rate of corporation tax and passed on to the lessee when received by the lessor.

Funding Considerations

When estimating the return on a proposed lease, the lessor will consider his own funding position in depth. For balance sheet purposes, equipment purchased for leasing has been considered to be a fixed asset, with the resulting loss of balance sheet liquidity. ED 29 ("Accounting for Leases"), published by the Accounting Standards Committee, recommends that lessors disclose their investment in finance leases separately, less the profit element allocated to future periods. The net investment is usually described as "investment in finance leases" or "rentals receivables". For a banking house which leases equipment this can have significant implications, because, as has been explained in other chapters, it is required by regulations to keep a certain portion of its assets in a liquid state.

So far as leasing is concerned, the old banking adage that "it is unwise to borrow short and lend long" still holds good, and so the prudent lessor seeks to match his flow of rental income with term borrowing whenever practicable. However, a feature of a tax-based lease cash flow is that the lessor's borrowing requirement is usually for a shorter period than the primary period, because of the impact of the benefit of tax allowances. Ideally, he will borrow at a fixed rate of interest, pitched sufficiently below the estimated return from the lease to show an acceptable profit and to compensate for the loss of liquidity. Sometimes imported equipment may be financed by fixed-term loans at favourable rates extended from the supplier country. In practice such matching may not always be possible and therefore the lessor may suffer when he borrows in this latter fashion if the cost of the money borrowed by the lessor subsequently rises above the yield from the lease (because he is forced to grant a lease with fixed rentals). It is possible, however, for a lessor significantly to reduce its exposure to movements in interest rates by matching funds during the period until the benefit of tax allowances is received, as subsequent fluctuations in interest rates have a very much less significant impact on the lessor's return.

Alternatively, a lease may be structured as a floating rate facility where the rentals are linked to a market cost of funds, such as LIBOR or the F.H.B.R. (Finance Houses Association Base Rate). In such cases, the lease terms provide for the rentals to be varied if the lessor's cost of funds differs from the assumed rate used in the original rental calculation.

Nature of Involvement of Accepting Houses

Against this background it is now possible to appreciate the three principal ways in which an accepting house can be involved in leasing. These are as follows:

(a) as a lessor in its own right, buying equipment on a customer's order and leasing it to that customer;

(b) as banker to companies whose business is equipment leasing;

(c) as manager, either of a syndicate of banks or other financial institutions, which act in partnership to purchase and lease high-value equipment to a lessee or as adviser to a corporate customer which wishes to shelter a portion of its tax liability by granting a lease to a third party.

Dealing first with the accepting house as a lessor in its own right, it is necessary to understand how a lease is set up in practice.

The Accepting House as Lessor

Many accepting houses have granted leases to existing customers.

Clearly, if a house has been acting for years, either as banker or as financial adviser, to an industrial company, it is extremely well placed to take an overall view of that company's business. If the customer is contemplating some degree of expansion or renewal of manufacturing plant, the accepting house can review the development plan and estimate the future cash flow. Usually the accepting house can confidently grant a lease of the equipment required.

On other occasions, a prospective lessee will approach an accepting house through another finance company or perhaps through a specialist broker of leases. The accepting house will need to satisfy itself regarding the integrity and sound financial condition of the prospective customer. It will examine balance sheets and profit and loss accounts for past trading periods and ask questions on the up-to-date position. It will take references from other banks and outside sources. It will then examine the merits of the operation for which the equipment is required and satisfy itself that the customer will be able to pay the lease rentals. At the same time, usually working in close collaboration with the customer, it will enter into negotiations with the manufacturer or supplier of the equipment to be leased on the terms of the supply contract for the equipment. These may well entail making one or more payments on account to the supplier or manufacturer before delivery, together with installation charges and the costs which may be involved in having representatives of the manufacturer instruct the customer's staff in the operation of the equipment.

The accepting house will, if necessary, require the lessee to obtain performance guarantees in respect of the equipment from the manufacturer. Perhaps the equipment – for example, a computer – will require regular maintenance by the maufacturer's specialist organisation and in such case a maintenance contract has also to be arranged. When all has been agreed with the manufacturer and/or supplier, the accepting house will agree the terms of a lease of the equipment with its prospective customer. Often a number of these important contractual phases will overlap, but usually only after all have been completed will the lease with the customer be signed and an order be placed with the manufacturer or supplier by the accepting house for the equipment. Inevitably, in some cases the equipment will already have been ordered by the lessee before the lease finance is in place. In such circumstances the lessor either renews the original purchase order, substituting itself for the lessee, or acquires title after delivery to the lessee (before the equipment has been brought into use).

Sometimes the equipment leased may or may not itself be adequate security for the accepting house. Generally speaking, those accepting houses which lease equipment tend to rely more on the financial strength of their customers than upon the equipment. This attitude accords with their principal role as bankers. Nevertheless, an accepting house will be concerned to ensure that it does not lose title in any way to its equipment and there are a number of ways in which this is done. For example, equipment which becomes a fixture in rented premises could be claimed by the landlord in certain circumstances and so the accepting house will obtain a written waiver from the landlord of his rights to do this. The ownership of a leased aircraft is recorded on the register of the country under whose flag the aircraft flies. Free-standing equipment will sometimes have a small place mark or similar mark on it indicating its ownership. These are a few examples only.

In addition to taking security on the equipment, an accepting house may require outside guarantees from third parties or other forms of security in respect of the lessee's good performance of its obligations.

During the period of the lease an accepting house will take steps to ensure that the equipment is adequately insured and provisions to this effect will be written into the terms of the lease. Similarly, the onus of maintenance of the equipment will by the terms of the lease be placed formally on the lessee.

The Accepting House as Lending Banker

Most accepting houses lend as bankers to companies whose principal business is leasing equipment. They assess each customer, employing normal banking techniques to ensure that their security is good and that the risk is generally acceptable. The terms on which they lend will be in keeping with prevailing market lending rates. Lending by accepting houses for fixed terms and at fixed rates of interest is uncommon. As with any bank lending, accepting houses will evaluate the strength of the borrower's contract and its degree of risk and charge the customer accordingly.

The Accepting House as Manager/Adviser

The accepting houses are essentially managers of funds rather than massive lenders over the long term. Syndicates are formed under the management of one or more accepting houses to lend important sums. As individual accepting houses regularly act as financial advisers to corporate customers, it was a logical development for the houses either to seek to manage syndicates of banks and other financial institutions, acting jointly to grant a "big ticket" lease, or alternatively to set up and manage facilities which corporate customers could use to shelter from their tax liability. Acting as a lessor manager, an accepting house will offer a client a range of services including arranging and managing the client's lease portfolio, providing funds and, if appropriate, guaranteeing the lessee's financial obligations under the lease.

The problems of setting up a partnership of institutions to act as lessor of a ship or an aircraft are complex. When an accepting house takes on the role of manager of a syndicate of lending bankers it acts in the overall interest of the lenders, dealing with the customer on all aspects of the loan, day-to-day business and security. The manager of a leasing syndicate must in addition be concerned with the tax position of the syndicate and perhaps, too, with the claiming of grants from government authorities.

Since this is not an exhaustive textbook on the techniques of leasing, it is not possible to refer in any detail to the particular problems of leasing complex equipment, such as ships, aircraft and computers. Generally speaking, however, the more sophisticated the equipment, the more attention must be paid to what may be described as operational considerations. The prudent lessor places itself in the position of the operator of the equipment and ascertains, so far as it can, the risks inherent in operating it. In drawing up the lease contract, it will seek to protect itself from the dangers that flow from any failure on the part of the lessee to take all steps necessary to diminish these risks. To give one example only, the lessor of an aircraft will at all times be most concerned that adequate insurance is in force to cover a wide range of passenger and third-party risks, in addition to the obvious requirement to insure the airframe and engines of the aircraft. The possibility of a catastrophic accident, such as an aircraft crashing into a major city, must be taken into account.

International Business

The foregoing paragraphs indicate the principal ways in which accepting houses are involved in equipment leasing in the United

Kingdom. Accepting houses, however, have always been international in their outlook and they may well have overseas leasing involvements as well as domestic ones. Many accepting houses have overseas subsidiaries and associates which may in their turn grant leases or invest in or lend funds to leasing companies in their own right. A few of the accepting houses, however, are prepared to grant "cross-border" leases.

In cross-border leasing the ownership of the asset is held by the lessor in one country while the leased asset may be physically located and operated in another. Once again, complex procedures are involved and an accepting house must be aware of the legal and fiscal position as it relates to leasing in the country where the asset is located and operated before it can consider the granting of a lease. Perhaps it will be agreed that rent may be paid in a foreign currency or the equipment purchased abroad. In either case, the considerations of a lessor when funding its purchase will be different from those applying to a domestic transaction. Doubtless the services of the accepting house's foreign money desk will be called for. Sometimes the accepting house will require its lessee to accept a series of bills of exchange, payable at future dates and in respect of each rental due. Since the *Finance Act,* 1982 the prospects for tax-based export leasing from the U.K. have been severely restricted.

Some Advantages and Disadvantages of Leasing

Various claims are made regarding the advantages and disadvantages of leasing from the standpoints of the lessor and the lessee. These vary from time to time with changing economic circumstances. They are too numerous to list here. Certain advantages for the lessor will have become apparent from earlier paragraphs. From the lessee's standpoint there are a number of important reasons for leasing, such as flexibility compared to other forms of finance. It is also a source of a medium-term, fixed-rate finance and an additional source of finance, but the underlying reason is usually cost, where the lessee is not in a position to take advantage of the tax-based investment incentives.

The Equipment Leasing Association

Most of the houses directly involved in leasing became members of the Equipment Leasing Association not long after it was formed in 1971. The Association, which is intended to promote the interests of lessors in the United Kingdom, provides a useful forum for them to discuss mutual problems.

Outlook

Since the early 1960s the use of equipment leasing has grown enormously. Many major companies now regularly lease the whole or part of their equipment and a wide range of equipment is covered. The total value of assets bought for leasing in the United Kingdom runs into thousands of millions of pounds. At the end of 1981 the cumulative costs of assets being leased within the primary period of leases granted by members of the Equipment Leasing Association was valued at £8,925 million, of which £2,674 million was attributable to assets acquired for leasing during 1981.

16

BULLION DEALING

Introduction and Definition

This chapter discusses the bullion-dealing activities transacted by banks as opposed to the activities of brokers connected with commodity exchanges such as the London Metal Exchange or the New York Comex Inc. In this context the term "bullion" refers to the precious metals: gold, silver and platinum. Widely traded precious metal coins should be added to the list of products normally dealt in by bullion dealers. Gold will be used to illustrate practical examples of bullion dealing in this chapter, but, of course, similar examples could be given using the other metals.

Dealing in bullion can conveniently be compared with foreign exchange dealing. As in the case of foreign exchange, dealing takes place in an international market. Professional dealers, although fewer in number than in the case of foreign exchange, quote bid and offered prices throughout the working day. Quotes are given for both spot and future settlement and apply to standard quantities and qualities of the commodity being traded. Unlike metal brokers, who normally act as agents, bullion dealers act as principals, buying and selling commodities for their own account, the quoted purchasing and selling price serving as the basis for settlement without the addition of commissions.

However, by contrast with foreign exchange, bullion dealing is characterised by additional factors: as a physical product, bullion takes various manufactured forms and can be delivered in any location. Premiums over or discounts under the price quoted for the standard product for delivery in a specific bullion market – say,

London – reflect supply of and demand for different forms of bullion or deliveries in other locations. These premiums and discounts do not normally exceed the corresponding cost of manufacturing, transport and insurance, etc., which would arise should, for instance, metal delivered in Frankfurt be moved to London, or should scrap metal be converted into good delivery bars. A further contrast with foreign exchange is that bullion dealing involves the establishment of physical storage and delivery facilities.

In gold bullion dealing it is particularly important to recognise this dual characteristic: gold is both a form of money (a currency) and a commodity. It may therefore reflect the volatility of the foreign exchange markets or the physical commodity markets or indeed both.

Supply of Bullion

Mining

Bullion dealers may either act as agents for, or buy directly from, primary producers. In some cases, however, mines use common sales organisations or surrender their production to government authorities who are responsible for marketing. In the case of gold over 70% of annual world production (approximately 1,300 tons) emanates from South Africa and Russia. The gold produced by the South African mines is sold by the South African Reserve Bank primarily in the London and Zürich gold markets. Russian gold is sold in the market mainly through the offices of a Russian state-owned bank which also acts as a bullion dealer in its own right.

Recycling

Precious metals used by industry, in jewellery or in coins are constantly refined and melted back into the standard product and therefore represent a secondary source of supply.

Existing Stocks

Existing stocks are substantial, especially in the case of gold, and represent a large multiple of new production. Some of these stocks remain in firm hands, but a significant proportion is constantly being turned over.

Central banks are major holders of gold. Their total reserves amount to more than 30,000 tons. In the second half of the 1970s official auctions of part of the holdings of the U.S. Treasury and the I.M.F. released significant quantities of gold in the markets. Since then, official sales have in general been made only by a limited number of countries when they are suffering an overall deterioration in their foreign currency reserves.

The public at large holds gold both for an investment and in the form of jewellery in quantities usually estimated to be comparable to those held by central banks.

Demand for Bullion

Industrial Demand

Most bullion dealers do not supply precious metals in the form required by industry, *i.e.* in wires, plates, tubes, solutions, etc. A number of specialised metal-processing firms convert bullion into these products. In the main, however, bullion dealers supply industrial groups, particularly in the case of gold and silver. To a certain extent, and especially in the case of metals such as platinum and palladium, industrial supplies are routed directly from the producers to the industrial users without dealers as intermediaries. However, industrial companies often buy their supplies from mines or specialised manufacturers, but simultaneously use bullion dealers for hedging operations.

Central Banks

Only gold remains among the precious metals used as reserve assets by monetary authorities and many of these now value their gold at levels approximate to that of the free market. Gold reserves of the Group of Ten countries now remain fairly constant, but in recent years a number of other countries which have enjoyed a strong performance on their current account have increased the proportion of gold in their reserves by purchases in the open market.

Investment Demand

Substantial quantities of precious metals in the form of both bullion and coins are sold to investors by bullion dealers and in some years more than one-third of the world's gold production may be absorbed by investors. In other years, however, a high gold price may stimulate significant "dis-hoarding".

Traded Forms of Bullion

Bars

Bullion is traded in standard bars of defined weight and fineness. The London gold market, for instance, uses as good delivery a standard 400-oz bar with a tolerance range of 350 to 430 oz per bar, whereas the London Gold Futures Market and the commodity markets in the United States deal in 100-oz or kilogramme bars. The fineness of gold contained in such bars is normally required to constitute at least 995 parts per 1,000. Monetary adjustments are made to take weight differences and higher purity into account.

Forward Contracts

Bullion dealers will either provide their own quotations for forward deliveries or deal in contracts of established futures exchange markets. Forward contracts tend not to give rise to physical bullion deliveries, but are cleared by contrary trans-actions before maturity. There is currently no regularly quoted forward market such as exists in the foreign exchange markets.

Coins

Bullion dealers trade in coins which are available in large quantities, normally on a wholesale basis. Examples of such coins include the British sovereign and the South African Krugerrand.

Restrictions on Bullion Trading

Bullion dealers may be subject to rules in their respective countries of residence. It was only in 1975 that residents of the United States were permitted to purchase gold freely and a similar freedom was not enjoyed in the United Kingdom until 1979 when exchange control was abolished. In other countries, for example, France, while residents may deal in gold, all such deals must be registered and restrictions on the import and export of gold are extremely rigorous.

Whether or not gold is subjected to exchange controls, it is frequently subjected to a sales tax or, as within the E.E.C., varying levels of value added tax.

Bullion Markets

Bullion markets are international. Dealers operating from anywhere in the world deal with one another using telex and tele-phone as means of communication. If one speaks of a particular market, say, the London market, it means that there are a number of bullion dealers constituting a "market" (the London "gold fixing", for example) and that their price quotations refer to "London good delivery" bars. For convenience, however, most international gold traders deal on a "Loco London" price basis and the majority of their transactions will be cleared over accounts held with the London market.

The London market is, of course, well known for its gold fixing. The members of the fixing are Mocatta & Goldsmid Limited, Sharps Pixley, N. M. Rothschild & Sons Limited, Johnson Matthey Bankers Limited and Samuel Montagu & Co. Limited. Rothschild and Samuel Montagu are accepting houses in their own right and Sharps Pixley Limited is the wholly owned subsidiary of a third – Kleinwort, Benson Limited. The "fixing" takes place twice daily at the offices of N. M. Rothschild & Sons Limited, who act as chairman. Each member of the gold market is represented. The representatives of the members are in direct communication with their dealing rooms, which in turn liaise with a large number of clients throughout the world. Each member may have a number of orders for the purchase and sale of gold. The unmatched quantity, *i.e.* the net demand or supply, will be brought to the fixing. The chairman of the fixing adjusts the price upwards or downwards according to the excess of demand over supply or vice versa and the members may in turn adjust their orders until an equilibrium price is found at which buyers and sellers are evenly matched. Exceptionally, a percentage reduction of buy or sell orders may be necessary to achieve a balance.

The advantage of the fixing is the narrow spread thus achieved between the buying and selling price. Sellers obtain the fixing price without any deduction, while buyers pay $1/4\%$ commission in addition to the fixing price. All deals are effected at the published fixing price. The fixing helps to bring temporary price stability to the international gold market, as it "matches" a high volume of orders from customers and bullion markets throughout the world. It also plays an important role for price determination in industrial contracts involving gold supplies and in the valuation of the official reserves of many countries.

In conjunction with the London Metal Exchange the members of the fixing created the London Gold Futures Market in 1982. The mechanics of this market are very similar to those in New York

(Comex) and Chicago (the International Money Market division of the Mercantile Exchange).

Other International Markets

Other major international physical markets are also established in Zürich, Frankfurt, Hong Kong and Singapore. Tokyo is of increasing importance, but has yet to establish itself as a "market-making" centre. Beirut used to enjoy a dominant position in the Middle East, but currently there is no major dealing centre within the region although, as an entity, it can continue to exert a significant influence upon the market.

Dealing Techniques

Spot Dealing

By spot dealing one understands dealing for physical delivery, normally within a two-day settlement period. In gold, a large proportion of dealing takes place in the spot market, unlike silver, for example, where a larger proportion is effected for future delivery.

Forward Dealing

A forward contract is a contract for future delivery. The price may stand at a premium (contango) or at a discount (backwardation) to the spot price. These premiums and discounts are a function of supply and demand patterns for immediate and future delivery and of financing cost. As physical stocks of precious metals exist in sufficient quantities, forward prices are generally at a premium to spot prices and thus principally reflect the cost of financing. Indeed, a forward contract can be created by (in the case of a forward sale) borrowing funds for the period of the forward contract, and using the proceeds of the borrowing to purchase spot metal which the dealer holds until maturity of the forward contract; at maturity delivery will be made against payment and the borrowing is then reimbursed with the sale proceeds. Forward contracts are used by commercial parties for hedging purposes or in order to fix the price of future supplies.

A dealer who quotes forward prices, assuming that he does not wish to carry an outright price risk, will cover his forward sale by either a matching forward purchase or, as mentioned before, by a matching spot purchase. In the latter case, his financing cost must be covered by the forward premium on the future sale.

A further attraction of forward contracts is that investors do not have to pay the whole amount of the contract value before maturity date. Normally, however, they would effect a matching sale (in the case of an initial forward purchase) before the maturity of the initial deal.

Arbitrage

Apart from buying and selling a commodity in the same physical state, at the same location, and for the same delivery date, dealers will take advantage of price variations between different forms of such commodity, different locations of delivery, different delivery dates, etc. This activity is known as arbitrage and provides the mechanism which ensures that prices always tend to remain related to one another. The limiting factors for price differences are the costs of converting one form of the commodity into another (say, scrap metal into good delivery bars), transport costs including insurance (for instance Zürich to London), financing cost (spot against forward transaction), etc.

Spot against Forward Operations

Dealers refer to this activity as "cash and carry" or "loan and deposit" business. Thus, a spot sale generates funds which can be placed on deposit until the maturity date of the forward purchase. Similarly, a spot purchase requires funds to be borrowed for the period of the forward contract. Dealers will enter into these transactions when, in the case of a spot sale coupled with a forward purchase, the interest receivable on the deposit exceeds the premium payable on the forward purchase and vice versa. In the case of a spot purchase/forward sale the premium earned on the forward sale should exceed the financing cost of the borrowing that is required. A further consideration is that in the case of a spot sale/forward purchase physical metal is required to settle the spot sale or short position. This metal may be borrowed from other dealers or clients. Alternatively, it may come from contrary operations previously entered into, whereby the dealer acquired physical metal by purchasing spot and selling forward.

Risks

Apart from the obvious risk arising from price exposure, particular attention should be given to those arising from the advancement of credit. Default by a counterparty might give rise to two sorts of credit risks.

Settlement

Settlement may be effected cash against delivery, in which case no risk should arise. In practice it is often the case that payment instructions have been given without evidence of delivery having been received or vice versa. In certain cases this is inevitable owing to time differences in different centres. In such cases it could occur that payment or delivery has already been effected when the counterparty defaults in settlement of his obligation. These risks must be monitored by effective delivery and settlement procedures.

Price Fluctuation

Even in the case of a spot deal, two days normally elapse before settlement takes place. In the period between contract and settlement, prices may fluctuate adversely. For instance, after gold has been sold at a particular price on the contract date, the price may have weakened before the settlement date arrives. Should the counterparty default, the bullion dealer would "close" the contract by selling at a loss to another counterparty. Such risks can be limited only by monitoring counterparties (*see* "Limits" below) or by obtaining a sufficiently large deposit by way of margin before entering into the contract (*see* "Margin administration" below).

Of course, further risks of loss arise in transport and delivery. In this respect administrative procedures and insurance should exclude the risk of loss.

Administration

Positions

As mentioned above, the monitoring and control of dealing positions is of utmost importance in limiting price risks. Prices can fluctuate rapidly and substantial dealing can be achieved in a short period of time. It is essential that these control systems result in updated information at frequent intervals.

Limits

Based on credit analysis of counterparties and also on past experience, limits should be established as to the volume and value of outstanding deals with any counterparty at any particular time. The limit administration normally takes place within the dealing room, so that prior to effecting a deal the existing risk exposure on a counterparty can be checked against his limit and confirmation received that a further deal will not cause the limit to be exceeded.

Margin Administration

In the case of forward deals or of spot deals which involve the extension of credit to the counterparty, dealers will often ask their counterparty to put up margin deposits on or before the contract date. Such deposits come in two forms: an original margin on the initial contract; and a variation margin which is called when the counterparty suffers an adverse price movement.

Delivery and Transport Procedures

In this context it is not necessary to go into the details of these procedures, but merely to point out that the dealing function normally ends when a dealer has recorded his transaction on a dealing ticket, which is then to be processed by the dealing administration. Normally, deals are reconfirmed with counterparties on the same day to avoid misunderstandings. They are checked and are then processed; contract notes and accounting entries represent the main functions of the processing department, which also handles physical storage, delivery, insurance, etc.

Unallocated and Allocated Storage

In the case of unallocated storage, counterparties who frequently deal with one another will, in most cases, avoid moving precious metals into specific vaults designated by the counterparty, but will use accounting entries to reflect their mutual bullion positions. To this end Nostro and Vostro accounts (similar to those used for cash relationships) are employed, in this case called "exchange accounts" or "pool accounts", which are maintained in terms of ounces. Bullion dealers therefore owe and are owed precious metals which have not been specifically segregated in any vault and therefore constitute bank obligations. This system of exchange accounts avoids the costly movement of precious metals and reduces administration.

In the case of allocated storage metal is physically segregated in a vault and the counterparty informed of the serial number, weight and fineness of bars allocated to him. The particular significance of allocated storage is that the bank acts in this case as a custodian of the customer's property. Exchange accounts involve a direct, unsecured obligation of the bank towards the customer.

Other forms of storage of precious metals may also be evidenced by warrants, certificates, vault receipts and the like.

Accounting

Bullion dealing involves specific accounting problems, especially so far as the valuation of future contracts is concerned, valuation being necessary whenever profits require to be assessed. The sort of problem which arises can be easily illustrated by a forward arbitrage operation where several currencies are concerned. A dealer may have bought and sold metal for delivery on different dates in the future and for settlement in different currencies. To avoid an exchange risk he would have effected forward foreign exchange transactions for the sale of the currency he expects to receive and for its conversion into the currency he will have to pay. Therefore, the valuation of metals positions will involve not only the positions themselves, but also foreign exchange positions, loans and deposits (if applicable), etc.

Conclusion

Bullion dealing is a particularly challenging area because it combines the aspects of dealing in a commodity with those of banking (foreign exchange, lending and borrowing, etc.). It is further complicated by its physical aspect, *i.e.* conversion (refining, manufacturing), transport, insurance and storage. The risks incurred in bullion dealing and the necessity for appropriate limits and control procedures have been noted. It is, however, important to facilitate dealing by sufficient freedom of action and flexibility of administrative systems, while precise and efficient administrative controls and procedures should limit risks to acceptable levels.

A comprehensive bullion-dealing activity facilitates the entry of an institution into what may be termed "bullion banking". As can be seen, this may include servicing the producer (by way of forward sales and medium-term finance), the central banker (through the provision of swap facilities) and the consumer (with whom consignments of metal are placed). The recent volatility of the market place has in itself been a powerful stimulant to such services.

17

ACCEPTING HOUSES AND THEIR INSURANCE LINKS

To the general public all merchant banks may look alike from a distance. Certainly the major and longer-established merchant banks (the accepting houses) have much in common, and yet a student of their affairs would be well advised to look closely at the ways in which they differ one from the other to understand how each has developed its own distinctive style of operations, capitalised on the opportunities that have presented themselves and generally (and happily) grown up in its own way.

The extent to which many of the accepting houses are linked with the world of insurance is an indication of their flexible attitudes towards providing different, but at the same time closely related, financial services for a profit. Yet the connections go further than this – today, for instance, we see the accepting houses owning insurance companies or insurance brokers and insurers owning stakes in accepting houses on a far greater scale than was ever visualised 20 or 25 years ago. Even the absence of any insurance link could be indicative in itself of a decision to resist diversification and to stick to the pure disciplines of traditional merchant banking.

However, to understand something of the reasons for this present complex skein of crossholdings and banking-insurance services one has to take into account the changes in the economic climate that occurred in the 1950s and the 1960s. Increasing world prosperity then created a challenge to the City to provide a wider range of financial services than ever before. The sharpening competition among the institutions was a natural challenge to the accepting houses.

The demand for capital for expansion by home and overseas industry, the need to provide new vehicles to manage the nation's growing savings and pension funds, steadily rising property prices, the quickening tempo of take-overs and mergers – all these factors compelled the accepting houses to study their own corporate development plans. Not the least important sign of the times was the fact that the once cumbrous clearing banks began to marshal their vast resources and invade territory previously regarded as merchant banking and insurance preserves.

Faced with problems of this kind, some accepting houses decided that it was in their best interests to remain small and specialised, with an outstanding reputation in their own field. Others elected to go for size and the broadest possible range of services to be available internationally.

Once the decision to enter insurance had been taken by those of the expansionist frame of mind, certain fundamental and fine judgements were necessary.

In the first place it has to be recognised that insurance is a bigger word than its three syllables may suggest. It covers an industry which is every bit as complex and diverse as banking. Within it is the important – although not always wholly clear – distinction between those who act as intermediaries (insurance brokers) and those who act as principals (insurance companies and underwriters). It calls for a wide range of specialist disciplines as sophisticated as any other sector of the City; it is international in character and contains its own specialist institutions – such as Lloyd's – with their own traditions and mores.

It is not surprising, therefore, that those accepting houses which have entered insurance have done so by a multiplicity of routes with varying motivations. Of course, it has to be assumed that increased profits were an objective common to all. Admittedly, it is just possible to argue that it could be in the interest of client relations to offer an insurance service at break-even or modest loss – but not for long. Any service industry can survive only if it is dynamic, innovative and purposeful, except in the rare instance when it has to be established as "client fodder". So far as the accepting houses are concerned, their involvement in insurance services could clearly not be treated as a loss leader; nor could such a situation be countenanced by insurance companies or insurance brokers.

Moreover, synergy in a diversified service company is not necessarily demanded by clients. Each service has to be offered and sold positively. Indeed, synergy, so far from being automatically a positive force, can sometimes create negative results. Bad service (real or alleged) in one area can automatically upset and lose clients in another. Good service does not automatically bring the reverse.

Recognising that the basic motivation was the profitable expansion of services, why then should insurance in one form or another have been chosen as a companion by so many accepting houses? There are probably five main reasons for this. In the first place, insurance, like banking, is a City activity familiar to the banking community because of its enormous financial muscle. Secondly, many insurance activities do not need increases in capital as they grow. Thirdly, the possibility of creating synergy does exist (all bank clients must have insurance cover of some sort). Fourthly, there are some aspects of insurance where the expertise of the accepting houses can be of direct value, as, for example, in the management of cash flow, an important ingredient of most insurance-broking business; in the investment of insurance and pension funds; and in the management of unit trusts, particularly when linked to life assurance policies. Fifthly, with the exception of general insurance companies, the insurance business tended to show consistent growth free from the cyclical pattern of merchant banking.

Thus it is that, within the broad picture of the insurance links of the accepting houses, insurance broking and life assurance companies predominate – with financial interests in general insurance companies more limited. The second broad division is between those which have developed links by acquisition and those which have created them organically. A third is between those which prefer to be involved with wholly owned groups and those which are content with major stakes.

There can be seen then, among the 16 accepting houses, extensive connections with insurance: many of the houses have subsidiary or associated companies operating as brokers and, among them, are some of the largest international broking companies – household names in the world of insurance. All these broking companies are important in their own right and together represent a considerable share of the London insurance-broking market.

Most of these relationships have developed as a result of acquisitions by the accepting houses of successful companies, previously often in the ownership of the founders and their families; but in one case a broking company bought a merchant bank which was a member of the Accepting Houses Committee and so reversed the normal pattern.

However, many houses have developed their insurance-broking interests, organically, as an extension of their general banking services and in response to the evident needs of their clients.

At least six accepting houses have financial links with insurance companies – but, as already noted, these are mainly life companies – and, finally, it should be mentioned that there are many directors of the accepting houses who are also directors of insurance companies. Indeed, a number of those companies have more than one accepting house represented on their boards.

In short, therefore, the accepting houses collectively have an influential position in the British insurance industry.

POSTSCRIPT

There have been many changes affecting the banking scene since the first edition of *Modern Merchant Banking* was published in 1976. The scene is always changing and the only certainty is that the merchant banks will continue to adapt with their traditional flexibility to the challenges of each succeeding era. Much change is the consequence of competition and of developments in the market place; other changes have been consequent on legislation – and both Brussels and Westminster have shown themselves increasingly active in intervening in the affairs of financial institutions. Within the changing banking scene as a whole, the image (and the reality) of the accepting houses will continue to be of banks which provide highly qualified advice within comparatively small organisations and a wide range of specialist financial services geared to the needs of their clients.

APPENDIX A

ACCEPTING HOUSES COMMITTEE

List of constituents

Baring Brothers & Co. Limited	8 Bishopsgate, London EC2N 4AE
Brown, Shipley & Co. Limited	Founders Court, Lothbury, London EC2R 7HE
Charterhouse Japhet p.l.c.	1 Paternoster Row, St Paul's, London EC4M 7DH
Robert Fleming & Co. Limited	8 Crosby Square, London EC3A 6AN
Guinness Mahon & Co. Limited	32 St Mary-at-Hill, London EC3P 3AJ
Hambros Bank Limited	41 Bishopsgate, London EC2P 2AA
Hill Samuel & Co. Limited	100 Wood Street, London EC2P 2AJ
Kleinwort, Benson Limited	20 Fenchurch Street, London EC3P 3DB
Lazard Brothers & Co. Limited	21 Moorfields, London EC2P 2HT
Samuel Montagu & Co. Limited	114 Old Broad Street, London EC2P 2HY

Morgan Grenfell & Co. Limited
23 Great Winchester Street,
London EC2P 2AX

Rea Brothers p.l.c.
36–37 King Street,
London EC2V 8DR

N. M. Rothschild & Sons Limited
New Court,
St Swithin's Lane,
London EC4P 4DU

J. Henry Schroder Wagg & Co.
Limited
120 Cheapside,
London EC2V 6DS

Singer & Friedlander Limited
21 New Street, Bishopsgate,
London EC2M 4HR

S. G. Warburg & Co. Limited
(incorporating Seligman
Brothers)
30 Gresham Street,
London EC2P 2EB

APPENDIX B

ISSUING HOUSES ASSOCIATION

List of members

Henry Ansbacher & Co. Limited
1 Noble Street, Gresham Street,
London EC2V 7JH

Arbuthnot Latham Bank Limited
Northgate House,
20–24 Moorgate,
London EC2R 6HH

Barclays Merchant Bank Limited
P.O. Box 188,
15–16 Gracechurch Street,
London EC3V 0BA

Baring Brothers & Co. Limited
8 Bishopsgate,
London EC2N 4AE

The British Linen Bank Limited
P.O. Box 49, 4 Melville Street,
Edinburgh EH3 7NZ

Brown, Shipley & Co. Limited
Founders Court, Lothbury,
London EC2R 7HE

Cayzer Limited
Cayzer House, 2 St Mary Axe,
London EC3A 8BP

Charterhouse Japhet p.l.c.
1 Paternoster Row, St Paul's,
London EC4M 7DH

Close Brothers Limited
36 Great St Helen's,
London EC3A 6AP

County Bank Limited	11 Old Broad Street, London EC2N 1BB
Credit Suisse First Boston Limited	22 Bishopsgate, London EC2N 4BQ
G. R. Dawes & Co. Limited	Neville House, 42–46 Hagley Road, Edgbaston, Birmingham B16 8PZ
Dawnay, Day & Co. Limited	Garrard House, 31 Gresham Street, London EC2V 7DT
Energy, Finance & General Trust Limited	Dauntsey House, 4B Frederick's Place, Old Jewry, London EC2R 8HN
The English Association Trust Limited	4 Fore Street, London EC2Y 5EH
Equity Capital for Industry	Leith House, 47–57 Gresham Street, London EC2V 7EH
E. T. Trust Limited	Bank House, The Paddock, Wilmslow Road, Handforth, Wilmslow, Cheshire SK9 3HQ
European Banking Co. Limited	150 Leadenhall Street, London EC3V 4PP
The Federated Trust Corporation Limited	1 Love Lane, London EC2V 7JJ
James Finlay Corporation Limited	10–14 West Nile Street, Glasgow G1 2PP
First National Industrial Trust p.l.c.	P.O. Box 505, St Alphage House, Fore Street, London EC2P 2HJ
Robert Fleming & Co. Limited	8 Crosby Square, London EC3A 6AN
Antony Gibbs & Sons Limited	3 Frederick's Place, Old Jewry, London EC2R 8HD

Granville & Co. Limited	27–28 Lovat Lane, London EC3R 8EB
Gray Dawes Bank p.l.c.	22 Bevis Marks, London EC3A 7DY
Gresham Trust p.l.c.	Barrington House, Gresham Street, London EC2V 7HE
Grindlay Brandts Limited	P.O. Box 280, 23 Fenchurch Street, London EC3P 3ED
Guinness Mahon & Co. Limited	32 St Mary-at-Hill, London EC3P 3AJ
Hambros Bank Limited	P.O. Box 3, 41 Bishopsgate, London EC2P 2AA
Hill Samuel & Co. Limited	100 Wood Street, London EC2P 2AJ
I.C.F.C. Corporate Finance Limited	91 Waterloo Road, London SE1 8XP
Ionian Securities Limited	92–94 Borough High Street, London SE1 1LL
Leopold Joseph & Sons Limited	31–45 Gresham Street, London EC2V 7EA
Kleinwort, Benson Limited	P.O. Box 560, 20 Fenchurch Street, London EC3P 3DB
Lazard Brothers & Co. Limited	21 Moorfields, London EC2P 2HT
Lloyds Bank International Limited	40–66 Queen Victoria Street, London EC4P 4EL
London & Yorkshire Trust Limited	Granville House, 2A Pond Place, London SW3 6QJ
Lothbury Assets Limited	1 Laurence Pountney Hill, London EC4R 0BA
Manufacturers Hanover Limited	8 Princes Street, London EC2P 2EN

Matheson & Co. Limited — Matheson House, 142 Minories, London EC3N 1QL

Minster Trust Limited — Minster House, Arthur Street, London EC4R 9BH

Samuel Montagu & Co. Limited — 114 Old Broad Street, London EC2P 2HY

Morgan Grenfell & Co. Limited — 23 Great Winchester Street, London EC2P 2AX

J. F. Nash & Partners Limited — 9 Station Road, Kettering, Northamptonshire NN15 7HY

National Commerical and Glyns Limited — 26 St Andrews Square, Edinburgh EH2 1AH

Noble Grossart Limited — 48 Queen Street, Edinburgh EH2 2NR

Orion Royal Bank Limited — 1 London Wall, London EC2Y 5JX

Rea Brothers p.l.c. — 36–37 King Street, London EC2V 8DR

N. M. Rothschild & Sons Limited — P.O. Box 185, New Court, St Swithin's Lane, London EC4P 4DU

Scandinavian Bank Limited — 2–6 Cannon Street, London EC4M 6XX

J. Henry Schroder Wagg & Co. Limited — 120 Cheapside, London EC2V 6DS

Singer & Friedlander Limited — 21 New Street, Bishopsgate, London EC2M 4HR

Standard Chartered Merchant Bank Limited — 33–36 Gracechurch Street, London EC3V 0AX

Standard Industrial Trust Limited — Shelley House, 3 Noble Street, London EC2V 7DL

S. G. Warburg & Co. Limited (incorporating Seligman Brothers) — 30 Gresham Street, London EC2P 2EB

EXTRACTS FROM THE 1970 ANNUAL REPORT OF THE CITY PANEL ON TAKE-OVERS AND MERGERS

A study on the use of confidential price-sensitive information

. . . This study was duly undertaken . . . on the basis of a detailed questionnaire, with no less than thirteen Merchant Banks, selected to represent a fair cross-section of the whole, and it was conducted with the co-operation of one of the Clearing Banks, and of two firms of London Stockbrokers active in the new issue market and was assisted by conversations which had taken place in a different context with two Finance Companies not members of the Issuing Houses Association but actively engaged in the field of take-overs and investment advising. Whilst those who assisted in the Panel's enquiries were assured that their anonymity would be preserved, the Panel was in fact given the very greatest co-operation in a spirit of completely frank discussion.

It is convenient to take the opportunity of this Annual Report to set out the Panel's general conclusions of the whole matter. Some thoughts on the question of security and prevention of "leaks" have also been included.

All the Merchant Banks and others concerned were involved in the possibility of some conflict of interest or of professional propriety in that they were all, to a greater or lesser extent, in possession of confidential information about the position of particular companies to which they acted as corporate advisers, or on whose Boards some member of the firm might sit, whilst they were also engaged as investment advisers to pension or other funds or to individual clients whose investment portfolios they managed. In all cases, therefore, the theoretical or indeed actual possibility existed that information gained in the one capacity, as for instance about an impending take-over transaction or about some alteration in a company's affairs or profitability, could be used with advantage in the other capacity in advising a sale or purchase of securities.

In no case was it suggested that the use of inside information of this kind in such a manner would be other than wholly improper: in every case measures of one kind or another had been taken to guard against the possibility.

. . . Except in the case of a few smaller Houses it is the fact . . . that all firms have created a certain physical segregation of the activities of corporate and of investment advising in that these matters are dealt with by separate individuals, in a distinct department, often on a different floor, sometimes in a different building and occasionally even through a distinct subsidiary company. . . .

Even where complete physical segregation is impracticable the general practice of all the larger Houses is that those persons below Board level who are concerned with the corporate advice activity and who may be aware of "inside" or "price-sensitive" information have no connection with or responsibility for the investment advice functions of that House. . . .

It is true that the existing practice in this country, as in the United States, does involve those concerned in the higher management of our Merchant Banks having dual capacities in which information received in the one is not to be used in the other. It may be claimed that this imposes an intellectual discipline on the individuals concerned which, however theoretically possible, it is quite impracticable to expect them to observe in every detail. And human fallibility and cupidity being what they are it is obviously impossible to guarantee that in every case this duality will not be abused. Yet the "wearing of two hats" is something which is accepted by all economically advanced societies and which in England is very far from limited to the merchant banking community. Wherever, whether in business, the professions or in public life, an individual stands in a confidential or sometimes even a judicial relationship to two or more interests, conflicts of interest of the kind canvassed here are bound to arise. In the vast majority of cases they are satisfactorily resolved. The risk of occasional abuse is far outweighed by the manifold advantages which would be lost if duality of this sort were prohibited. . . .

The fact is of course that in the context of take-overs those who are in possession of inside information will include directors of the companies involved, some at least of the financial, legal and secretarial departments of those companies, often outside accountants and solicitors and stock-brokers and officials of Government Departments concerned, and in later stages printers, the Panel executives and the Quotations Department of The Stock Exchange. These far outnumber those involved in the Merchant Banks and if "leaks" occur, it by no means follows that they originate from the Merchant Banks. . . .

It was axiomatic in the case of every firm and individual who assisted in our enquiry that "inside" or confidential information obtained in the corporate advising capacity was not to be used in the capacity of investment advising, still less in the personal investments of the firm or individuals concerned. This rule is generally recognised and accepted by the clients of either department. In order to avoid the risks of mistake or abuse, the two functions are as far as practicable physically segregated in different departments and are the concern of separate executives. It is only those at director or partner level, or at the least senior executives of long experience and proven responsibility, who can or may have to operate in a dual capacity. There is some difference of practice in the case where knowledge of an imminent take-over transaction exists. Some Houses put the securities affected on a stop list so that all transactions in these by the Investment Department other than those ordered apparently in good faith by outside clients are precluded. This practice may lead to the suspicion that "something is afoot" and may be unfair to investment clients who have left the management of their portfolios at discretion to be exercised by reference to ordinary investment criteria. Other Houses permit transactions to proceed normally but insist with special strictness that no information not available with normal diligence to the ordinary investment analyst or stockbroker should be taken into account and that each transaction must be capable of clear and public justification by reference to ordinary investment criteria. . . .

For the information of the public it may be useful to state the following principles as ones which are generally observed in the City and are enjoined upon all who may in future engage in corresponding activities.

1. Clients of Corporate Advisory and of Investment Advisory Departments should be made aware of the existence of the other Departments and understand that in order to avoid conflict of interest these activities are confidential and segregated and they cannot expect to receive any advantage nor need fear any disadvantage from the fact that the House conducts both.

2. Privileged price-sensitive information which a House may hold about a company which is a client or on whose Board some member of the House may sit may not in any case be taken into account for the purpose of forming an investment decision.

3. Special knowledge available to a House about a client company or one upon whose Board some member of the House may sit is only to be used for the purpose of forming investment decisions if it is or would be equally available to an independent investment analyst or stockbroker upon reasonable enquiry from the company or other sources.

4. Whilst (subject to the rules of the Code) Houses are not precluded during the public transaction of a take-over from purchasing for their own account securities of a company for which they are acting, they must not purchase such securities for their discretionary investment clients except by reference to ordinary investment criteria and in no case simply to support the market in their client company's shares. Nor may they in advance of the public announcement of a take-over advise investment clients to accumulate shares in the offeree company in order to secure acceptance of the offer.

5. Equally, however, investment clients need not necessarily be deprived of the advantage of transactions based on ordinary market criteria simply because the House is acting for a party to the take-over transaction, although it is realised that some Houses prefer to operate a stop list system.

6. The number of persons in the House made privy to an impending take-over transaction or other confidential or price-sensitive information should be as restricted as practicable.

7. Houses should periodically review their security arrangements.

8. Houses should prohibit members of their staffs from dealing in any securities on their own account except through the House itself.

9. The standard by which the propriety and therefore permissibility of any proposed line of action in relation to deals in securities (the subject of price-sensitive information or of a take-over transaction) is to be judged is whether the House is prepared subsequently to justify at a public enquiry the action taken.

LONDON DISCOUNT MARKET ASSOCIATION

List of members

Alexanders Discount p.l.c.	1 St Swithin's Lane, London EC4N 8DN
Cater Allen p.l.c.	1 King William Street, London EC4N 7AU
Clive Discount Co. Limited	1 Royal Exchange Avenue, London EC3V 3LU
Gerrard & National Discount p.l.c.	32 Lombard Street, London EC3V 9BE
Gillett Brothers Co. p.l.c.	65 Cornhill, London EC3V 3PP
Jessel, Toynbee p.l.c.	30 Cornhill, London EC3V 3LH
King & Shaxson p.l.c.	52 Cornhill, London EC3V 3PD
Page & Gwyther Limited	1 Founders Court, Lothbury, London EC2R 7DB
Gerald Quin, Cope & Co. Limited	19–21 Moorgate, London EC2R 6BX
Seccombe, Marshall & Campion p.l.c.	7 Birchin Lane London EC3V 9DE

Smith, St Aubyn & Co. Limited   2 White Lion Court,
                                       London EC3V 3PN

The Union Discount Company of   39 Cornhill,
  London p.l.c.   London EC3V 3NU

APPENDIX E

SUGGESTIONS FOR FURTHER READING

Acres, W. M. *The Bank of England from within, 1694–1900* (London, 1931)

Bank of England. *Money for business* (London, 1978)

Bank of England. *Money for exports* (London, 1979)

Cowles, V. *The Rothschilds: a family of fortune* (London, 1973)

Ellinger, B. *The City: the London financial markets* (London, 1940)

Ellis, A. *Heir of adventure: the story of Brown, Shipley & Co., merchant bankers 1910–1960* (London, 1960)

Farrer, D. *The Warbugs* (London, 1975)

Feis, H. *Europe: the world's banker, 1870–1914* (New Haven, 1930)

Gibbs, J. A. *Merchants and bankers: a brief record of Antony Gibbs & Sons and its associated houses' business during 150 years: 1808–1958* (London, 1958)

Giuseppi, J. *The Bank of England: a history from its foundation in 1694* (London, 1966)

Hidy, R. W. *The House of Baring in American trade and finance: early English merchant bankers at work, 1763–1861* (Cambridge, Massachusetts, 1949)

Hoyt, E. P. *The House of Morgan* (London, 1963)

Issuing Houses Association. *British issuing houses* (London, 1974)

Jenks, L. H. *The migration of British capital to 1875* (London, 1938)

McRae, H. and Cairncross, F. *Capital City: London as a financial centre* (London, 1974)

Nevin, E. and Davis, E. W. *The London clearing banks* (London, 1970)

Perry, F. E. *Elements of banking* (London, 1981)

Powell, E. T. *The evolution of the money market 1385–1915* (London, 1916)

Pringle, R. *Banking in Britain* (London, 1973)

Radcliffe Report. *Report of the Committee on the Working of the Monetary System* (Chairman: Lord Radcliffe), Cmnd. 827 (London, 1959)

Reid, Sir Edward J. *The role of the merchant banks today*, Presidential Address to the Institute of Bankers (London, 1963)

Sayers, R. S. *Modern banking*, 7th edition (Oxford, 1967)

Truptil, R. J. *British banks and the London money market* (London, 1936)

Wechsberg, J. *The merchant bankers* (London, 1967)

Wilson Report. *Report of the Committee to Review the Functioning of Financial Institutions* (Chairman: Sir Harold Wilson), Cmnd. 7937 (London, 1980)

Young, G. K. *Merchant banking: practice and prospects*, 2nd edition (London, 1971)

INDEX

146